Connections

Worship
Companion

ALSO AVAILABLE IN THIS SERIES

Connections Worship Companion: Year C, Volume 1
Connections Worship Companion: Year C, Volume 2

Connections

Worship
Companion

David Gambrell, editor

WESTMINSTER
JOHN KNOX PRESS
LOUISVILLE · KENTUCKY

First Edition
Published by Westminster John Knox Press
Louisville, Kentucky

22 23 24 25 26 27 28 29 30 31—10 9 8 7 6 5 4 3 2 1

Book design by Drew Stevens
Cover design by Allison Taylor

Library of Congress Cataloging-in-Publication Data

Names: Gambrell, David, editor.
Title: Connections worship companion : Year C / David Gambrell.
Description: First edition. | Louisville, Kentucky : Westminster John Knox
  Press, 2021. | Series: Connections: a lectionary commentary for
  preaching and worship | Includes index. | Summary: "Part of the
  Connections commentary series, these worship resources help
  congregations illuminate the connections between Scripture and
  liturgical rhythms. A "Making Connections" essay precedes each
  liturgical season's resources, providing context for worship within the
  themes and purpose of the season"-- Provided by publisher.
Identifiers: LCCN 2021023009 (print) | LCCN 2021023010 (ebook) | ISBN
  9780664264963 (hardback) | ISBN 9781646982080 (ebook)
Subjects: LCSH: Common lectionary (1992). Year C. | Public worship. |
  Worship programs.
Classification: LCC BV199.L42 C66 2021 (print) | LCC BV199.L42 (ebook) |
  DDC 264.05--dc23
LC record available at https://lccn.loc.gov/2021023009
LC ebook record available at https://lccn.loc.gov/2021023010

Connections Worship Companion, Year A, Volume 1
ISBN: 9780664264925 (hardback)
ISBN: 9781646982820 (ebook)

Contents

Introduction

This is not a book of prayers—
at least not yet.

These words will not become prayers
until the Holy Spirit breathes them,
until the body of Christ speaks and hears them,
until the people of God live them
in acts of service and love.

These words come from different people
in different places of ministry—
pastors and poets,
students and scholars,
activists and artists,
evangelists and educators,
bakers and baristas,
mission workers and musicians.

They have different voices,
and those voices will resonate
with different worshipers
in different ways.

It will be up to you,
as a planner and leader of worship,
to make these words sing:

to pray them
among the beloved people of God
with honesty, passion, wonder, and grace;

to enact them
as the whole body of Christ
with heart, mind, soul, and strength;

to transform them
through the gifts of the Spirit,
with rhythm, color, texture, and taste.

You are encouraged, then,
even challenged,
even required
to find your own voice,
to inhabit these texts,
to adapt them as needed,
so that these words
may become the prayers
of your people
in your place
for the sake of the world,
all people,
in every place.

Only then
will these words become prayers.

Only then
will they rise like incense before God,
joining the intercession
of our great high priest,
Christ Jesus,
who still teaches us to pray.

David Gambrell

How to Use This Book

Three kinds of materials are provided in this volume. First, at the beginning of each major section is a short essay titled "Making Connections." These brief passages of commentary have several purposes:

- they introduce the primary theological themes of a given time in the Christian year;
- they highlight a particular biblical text, drawn from the lectionary, that may be used as a kind of lens for magnifying and examining the themes of the season;
- they point to distinctive features of the lectionary cycle included in this volume; and

- they offer practical and pastoral guidance for leaders as they seek to prepare faithful, thoughtful, creative, and engaging worship for the people of God.

These essays can be used in discussion with worship committees, planning teams, or church staff groups to promote biblical study, inspire theological reflection, and inform liturgical action.

Second, each section includes a collection of seasonal/repeating resources. These are liturgical texts intended for use during a certain span of time in the Christian year, whether occasionally or for several weeks in a row. Specifically, these resources include the following acts of worship:

> Confession and Pardon
> Prayer for Illumination
> Thanksgiving for Baptism
> Great Thanksgiving
> Prayer after Communion
> Prayer of Thanksgiving (for the dedication of the offering when the Eucharist is not celebrated)
> Blessing

These texts are somewhat broader and more general in their theological content and liturgical language, and they are designed for multiple uses within a liturgical season or period of Ordinary Time. They promote diachronic (meaning "through time") connections from one Sunday to the next, deriving their benefit from regular engagement with the church's tradition as people return to worship from week to week. They emphasize central convictions of Christian faith and life, supporting the kind of faith formation that takes place through sustained, long-term participation in worship. These texts are especially connected with the celebration of the sacraments.

Third, there is a set of resources for each Sunday or festival in the Christian year. Specifically, these resources include the following elements of the service:

> Opening Sentences (or Call to Worship)
> Prayer of the Day (or Gathering Prayer)
> Invitation to Discipleship
> Prayers of Intercession
> Invitation to Offering
> Invitation to the Table
> Charge

These texts are somewhat narrower and more specific in their theological content and liturgical language, and they are designed for use on a given Sunday or festival in the Christian year. They promote synchronic (meaning "same time") connections between the liturgy and the lectionary, deriving their benefit from flashes of insight that collect around a common word, image, or phrase from the biblical texts for the day. They emphasize particular practices of Christian faith and life, supporting the kind of faith formation that takes place in more concentrated, short-term experiences of worship. These texts are especially connected with the proclamation of the word.

By combining the **seasonal/repeating resources (in bold type)** with the *Sunday/festival elements (in italics)*, as well as other elements not provided in this resource (in regular type), as indicated below, worship planners will be able to assemble complete orders of worship for the Lord's Day.

GATHERING

Opening Sentences
Hymn, Psalm, or Spiritual Song
Prayer of the Day
Confession and Pardon

WORD

Prayer for Illumination
Scripture
Sermon
Hymn, Psalm, or Spiritual Song
Affirmation of Faith
Invitation to Discipleship
Thanksgiving for Baptism
Prayers of Intercession

EUCHARIST   [IF THE EUCHARIST IS OMITTED]

Invitation to Offering	*Invitation to Offering*
Offering	Offering
Invitation to the Table	
Great Thanksgiving	**Prayer of Thanksgiving**
Communion	
Prayer after Communion	

SENDING

Hymn, Psalm, or Spiritual Song
Blessing and *Charge*

This order of worship is offered as one example. The actions and elements of worship may of course be arranged in a variety of other ways according to denominational patterns and congregational practices. This resource is also available in ebook format, from which users can copy and paste liturgies for use in bulletins and other worship materials.

Lectionary Readings

This resource is designed to support and equip users of the three-year Revised Common Lectionary (1992), developed by the ecumenical Consultation on Common Texts as an adaptation and expansion of the Common Lectionary (1983). The contents and composition of this volume reflect that emphasis, consistent with the Connections commentary series.

However, this resource also includes supplemental liturgical materials for the four-year Narrative Lectionary (2010), designed by faculty at Luther Seminary in St. Paul, Minnesota. Taking advantage of overlap between the two systems, with these supplemental materials, this resource will address (at least obliquely) all of the primary texts of the Narrative Lectionary over the course of its six volumes.

See the Scripture index for the list of the lectionary readings supported in this volume (in canonical order). A comprehensive biblical index for both lectionaries will be published when all six volumes of the *Connections Worship Companion* have been completed.

Acknowledgments

Contributors to this volume include Claudia L. Aguilar Rubalcava, Mamie Broadhurst, Marci Auld Glass, Marcus A. Hong, Kimberly Bracken Long, Emily McGinley, Samuel Son, Slats Toole, and Byron A. Wade. Their deep faith, pastoral wisdom, creative gifts, and fervent prayers are the lifeblood of this work. The editor also expresses deep gratitude to David Maxwell, vice president for curriculum and church resources at Westminster John Knox Press, for his guidance in the development of this project, and to Jessica Miller Kelley, senior acquisitions editor at Westminster John Knox Press, for shepherding it to completion.

Key to Symbols and Abbreviations

Regular	Leader
Bold	People
Italics	Rubric describing liturgical action or identifying options
. . .	Time for individual prayers, spoken or silent
or	Alternate readings or responses

Resources for the Revised Common Lectionary

SEASON OF ADVENT

Making Connections

The season of Advent is a time of endings and beginnings. Advent begins by looking forward to the end—the culmination of God's saving work, the coming of a new creation, and the return of Christ to reign in glory. Advent ends by returning to the beginning—a fresh chapter in the story of salvation, the opening words of the Gospels, and the birth of Jesus the Messiah. The thread that holds all these themes together is the promise of the presence of God.

The Gospel of Matthew, featured in Year A of the Revised Common Lectionary, begins and ends with the promise of God's presence in Jesus Christ. In the first chapter of Matthew, an angel of the Lord announces to Joseph that Mary's child will be called "'Emmanuel,' which means 'God is with us'" (Matt. 1:23); these words are read on the Fourth Sunday of Advent, Year A, just as the season of Advent comes to its conclusion. In the final chapter of Matthew, the risen Lord tells the disciples, "Remember, I am with you always, to the end of the age" (Matt. 28:20); this promise is proclaimed on Trinity Sunday, Year A, as the second half of the Christian year commences. Thus, the promise of God's presence has a special significance in the way it is woven into the first Gospel and this lectionary year.

As the church begins its year with the Gospel of Matthew, be attentive to the theological themes of promise and presence as they appear throughout the Gospel—from the opening genealogy to the closing Great Commission. Be mindful also of the ways in which they are manifest in Christian liturgy and Christian life—especially through the proclamation of the word, the celebration of the sacraments, and the everyday patterns of prayer and spiritual disciplines that sustain us from Sunday to Sunday.

During the season of Advent, there are ample opportunities to connect the promises of God through the prophets to the concerns and challenges of our present age. The readings from Isaiah have particularly strong implications for peacemaking, social justice, ministries of compassion, and the care of creation. The readings from Matthew begin with the *challenge* of Jesus' presence to those who are unprepared for his coming, turning in the final week of Advent to the *comfort* of his presence as Emmanuel and

Savior. Three readings from Romans complement the themes of promise and presence while anticipating an extended engagement with this epistle in the time after Pentecost.

Trust this promise: God is with you. Know this presence: God is with you. The one who has loved you from the beginning will meet you at the end.

Seasonal/Repeating Resources

These resources are intended for regular use throughout the season of Advent.

CONFESSION AND PARDON

The confession and pardon may be led from the baptismal font.

> Now is the time to wake from sleep—
> to cast off the shroud of sin
> and put on the garment of grace.
>
> Let us trust the promise of God's mercy,
> for the day of salvation is near.

The confession may begin with a time of silence for personal prayer.

> **God of the ages,**
> **through the prophets and apostles**
> **you have challenged us**
> **to lay aside the works of destruction**
> **and prepare for your new creation.**
> **We confess that we continue**
> **to cling to our sinful ways—**
> **greed and lust,**
> **abuse and waste,**
> **envy and strife.**
>
> **Forgive us, Holy One.**
> **By your Spirit, lead us to live**
> **in a way that honors you,**
> **proclaiming the good news**
> **of Jesus Christ our Savior,**
> **who is coming in glory to reign.**

Water may be poured or lifted from the baptismal font.

> Through the gift of baptism
> we are cleansed in the Holy Spirit,
> clothed with the righteousness of Christ,
> and covered by the grace of God.

> Believe the good news:
> In the name of Jesus Christ, we are forgiven.
> **Thanks be to God.**

PRAYER FOR ILLUMINATION

The prayer for illumination is led from the lectern or pulpit.

> Faithful God,
> through the gift of your word
> you offer us instruction,
> encouragement, and hope.
> By the power of your Spirit
> teach us to live in hope,
> sharing joy and peace with the world;
> in the name of Jesus our Lord. **Amen.**

THANKSGIVING FOR BAPTISM

The thanksgiving for baptism is led from the baptismal font.

The introductory dialogue ("The Lord be with you . . .") may be sung or spoken.

> We give you thanks, O God,
> for the blessing of baptism—
> water in the wilderness
> and streams in the desert;
> healing for the thirsty earth
> and hope for hungry souls.
> Continue to shower upon us
> the gifts of your Holy Spirit.
> Strengthen us in our weakness,
> and take away our trembling.
> Lead us on the homeward path,
> and teach us the heavenly song
> of everlasting joy and gladness;
> through Jesus Christ our Lord. **Amen.**

GREAT THANKSGIVING

The Great Thanksgiving is led from the Communion table.

In this eucharistic prayer, the responsive phrases ("Here we lift our hearts . . .") may be replaced with a musical setting of "O Come, O Come, Emmanuel" or with sung or spoken versions of the introductory dialogue ("The Lord be with you . . ."), the Sanctus ("Holy, holy, holy . . ."), a memorial acclamation ("Christ has died . . ."), and a Trinitarian doxology and Great Amen.

> Here we lift our hearts to you,
> praying: Come, Lord Jesus!
> **O come, O come, Emmanuel!**
>
> All glory and honor to you, O Lord,
> for the promise of your saving love—
> new life and hope springing forth
> from the stump of Jesse's tree;
> a world where wolf and lamb,
> leopard and kid, lion and calf
> will live together in safety and peace
> and a little child will lead us.
> Here we lift our hearts to you,
> praying: Come, Lord Jesus!
> **O come, O come, Emmanuel!**
>
> All glory and honor to you, O Lord,
> for by your grace you sent us a Savior—
> one who delights in worshiping you
> and brings equality and justice
> to people who are humble and poor,
> one who has destroyed the power of death
> and will be faithful and righteous forever.

The words of institution are included here, if not elsewhere, while the bread and cup are lifted (but not broken/poured).

> Remembering your promises
> and rejoicing in your presence,
> we offer the sacrifice of praise.
> Here we lift our hearts to you,
> praying: Come, Lord Jesus!
> **O come, O come, Emmanuel!**

All glory and honor to you, O Lord,
for the gift of your Holy Spirit—
the Spirit of wisdom and understanding,
the Spirit of counsel and might,
the Spirit of knowledge and wonder.
Pour out your Spirit upon us
and upon this heavenly banquet
until the earth is full of your glory
like the waters that cover the sea.
Here we lift our hearts to you,
praying: Come, Lord Jesus!
O come, O come, Emmanuel!

PRAYER AFTER COMMUNION

The prayer after Communion is led from the Communion table.

Good and gracious God,
as you have been with us
at this holy meal,
be with us in our daily bread.
Help us to be with others
in the name of the one who says,
"I am with you always,"
Jesus Christ, Emmanuel. **Amen.**

PRAYER OF THANKSGIVING

The prayer of thanksgiving may be led from the Communion table.

Blessed are you, O Lord our God,
for you have done wondrous things.
Your glory fills the whole earth.
You send the rain to water the land
and cause the fields to flourish.
You defend those who are poor
and deliver those who are oppressed.
Use the works of our hands
to establish your holy realm,
and strengthen our hearts
as we wait for the coming
of Jesus Christ our Lord. **Amen.**

BLESSING

The blessing and charge may be led from the doors of the church.

May the God of steadfast love
lead you forth in harmony.
May the Lord of everlasting life
welcome you into glory.
May the Spirit of abounding hope
fill you with joy and peace. **Alleluia!**

First Sunday of Advent

Isaiah 2:1–5 Romans 13:11–14
Psalm 122 Matthew 24:36–44

OPENING SENTENCES

The prophet Isaiah
made this invitation to his listeners,
and he extends it to us again today:
Come, let us go up
to the mountain of the Lord.
Let us go to the house
of the God of Jacob and Rachel.
May God teach us
to walk in God's paths.

Let us worship God.

PRAYER OF THE DAY

God of yesterday, today, and tomorrow,
God of the beginning and the end times:
As we begin this journey through Advent
and start a new year in our Christian story,
we remember that your time is different from our time.
We must stay awake and pay attention
because your peace is not our peace,
and your ways are not our ways.
We do not know the hour or the day
when you are coming,
but we know that we must be watchful
for all the ways you will appear.
Even as we remember this beginning,
we know that you will be with us to the end.
With hope, peace, joy, and love we pray. **Amen.**

INVITATION TO DISCIPLESHIP

The invitation to discipleship may be led from the baptismal font.

In times of uncertainty,
when new things are just beginning
or when we cannot see the end,
we are invited to put our trust in God;
we are invited to be ready for anything.
We may not know what will happen next,
but we know we will not be alone.

This week, how can you reach out to someone
to let them know they are not alone?
How will you remember that God is with you?

PRAYERS OF INTERCESSION

The prayers of intercession may be led from the midst of the congregation.

God of hope,
we come to you as our waiting time begins—
this "already but not yet" time.
We look forward just a few weeks
and prepare to celebrate your coming years ago.
We remember to prepare for your coming again.
We pray in hope.

God of peace,
as part of the preparation for your coming,
may we begin to beat our swords into plowshares.
May we dismantle our weapons of mass destruction,
and rid ourselves of our stockpiles of fear.
May we sow seeds of connection rather than discontent.
May we teach peace to the nations
who continue to study war, including our own.
We pray for your peace.

God of joy,
lead us in the joyful work of making peace.
May we seek ways to feed those who hunger,
to bind up those who are wounded,
to get treatment for all who are addicted,
to find housing for all who need it,
and provide protection for any who are not safe.
May our joy be rooted in your promises
to care for the stranger,
to release the captive,
to bring good news to the poor,
and to let the oppressed go free.
We pray for such joy.

God of love,
a joy so deep and wide will surely expand our hearts.
So today as we pray for those we love already—
family, friends, neighbors, colleagues—
we pray also for those who are harder for us to love—
family, friends, neighbors, colleagues.
Love isn't easy,
so we ask for your strength and guidance.
We pray to love well.

As we journey toward Bethlehem
to meet you at the manger once again,
may we not forget to look for you
all around and at all times—
wherever we encounter
your hope, peace, joy, and love.
In Jesus' name we pray. **Amen.**

INVITATION TO OFFERING

The invitation to offering may be led from the Communion table.

In the season of Advent we remember
that God came as a gift to and for us.
As we enter this season of preparation,
may we bring our own gifts to and for God.

INVITATION TO THE TABLE

The invitation to the table is led from the Communion table.

Just as Advent invites us
to look forward and to look back,
this table does as well.
We look back to all the meals Jesus shared
with all the different people
in all the different places.
This table offers us a chance
to share a meal with Jesus today,
but it also points us to the final table—
a table at the end of time
where there will be a feast for all,
with no swords or spears,
no quarreling and jealousy.

At this table we come to taste
the hope, peace, joy, and love of Christ,
and to imagine a world in which
we know it all completely.
Come to the table.

CHARGE

The blessing and charge may be led from the doors of the church.

The psalmist writes,
"For the sake of the house of the Lord our God,
I will seek your good."
As we go forth in this new church year,
preparing to celebrate God's birth into this world,
let us go out and seek the good of others.
Amen. *or* **Thanks be to God.**

Worshipers may be invited to say to one another, "I will seek your good."

Second Sunday of Advent

Isaiah 11:1–10
Psalm 72:1–7, 18–19

Romans 15:4–13
Matthew 3:1–12

OPENING SENTENCES

Prepare the way of the Lord!
Prepare the way of the Lord!

Rejoice and clear the path,
for God is coming!
Prepare the way of the Lord!

PRAYER OF THE DAY

God of the wolf and the lamb,
God of the goat and the leopard,
we gather here to worship you—
you who bring enemies together,
you who combine earth and heaven,
you who know nothing of impossibility.
Expand our hopes and our imaginations
so that new dreams
of peace and unity might arise.
May the hearing of your word,
the singing of sacred songs,
and the blessing of this community
awaken us anew to your presence.
With hope, peace, joy, and love we pray. **Amen.**

---

*The wolf shall live with the lamb, the leopard shall lie down
with the kid, the calf and the lion and the fatling together,
and a little child shall lead them.*

Isaiah 11:6

INVITATION TO DISCIPLESHIP

The invitation to discipleship may be led from the baptismal font.

John the Baptist exhorts us
to prepare the way of the Lord.
But what does that mean?
We are to be messengers of peace and unity,
speaking truth to power.
But how do we do that?
Sometimes all of that seems just as impossible
as a lion bedding down with an ox
or a cow grazing with a bear.
But this is a season of impossible things.

Pick something "impossible" to work on this week,
and take just one step toward it,
remembering the Advent promise
that God—Emmanuel—is with us.

PRAYERS OF INTERCESSION

The prayers of intercession may be led from the midst of the congregation.

God of the universe and God of small things,
today we take a break
from worrying about life's extremes.
Today we remember
that everything comes together in you,
and we do not have to understand how that can be.

We pray for our friends
and for our enemies.
We pray for those we understand
and for those who confound us.
We pray for the rich and for the poor,
for our neighbors and strangers in our midst.
We pray for the vulnerable
and for those with great power.
We trust you to know all these prayers
and how to fulfill them.

God of steadfastness and encouragement,
show us how to live in harmony
and call out vipers when we see them.
Give deliverance to the needy, and crush the oppressor,
even as we are among their number.
Let the mountains yield prosperity for the people,
even as we hold an axe to the root of the trees.
Guide us through the eyes of these needles,
that righteousness may flourish and peace abound.

We lift to you the things that bring us joy . . .
We carry to you the weight of all our sorrows . . .
We trust you to hold these dear—
in celebration and in sadness.

As we journey toward Bethlehem
to meet you at the manger once again,
help us to know that you are with us
from the beginning to the end.
In Jesus' name we pray. **Amen.**

INVITATION TO OFFERING

The invitation to offering may be led from the Communion table.

We give thanks for the bustling brightness of the day
and for the delicious darkness of the night.
We sit amazed at the vastness of the ocean
and the universe within a raindrop.
These gifts show us the value
of gifts both great and small.

Let us share the gifts we have
with thanksgiving and delight.

INVITATION TO THE TABLE

The invitation to the table is led from the Communion table.

Jew or Gentile, slave or free,
wolf or lamb, child or viper,
poor or rich, red or blue—
all are welcome at this table.

We have brought the bread and cup,
but it is Christ who invites us to eat our fill,
Christ who encourages us to slake our thirst.
Come to the table.

CHARGE

The blessing and charge may be led from the doors of the church.

Repent, for the kingdom of heaven has come near!
Praise God and rejoice!
Prepare the way of the Lord.
Bear fruit worthy of repentance.
And may the God of hope
fill you with all joy and peace in believing,
so that you may abound in hope
by the power of the Holy Spirit.
Amen. *or* **Thanks be to God.**

Third Sunday of Advent

Isaiah 35:1–10
Psalm 146:5–10
 or Luke 1:46b–55

James 5:7–10
Matthew 11:2–11

OPENING SENTENCES

The divisions suggested here may be adapted for different contexts.

Happy are those
whose help is the God of Jacob,
whose hope is in the Lord their God,

[left side] **who made heaven and earth,
the sea, and all that is in them;**
[right side] **who keeps faith forever;**
[left side] **who executes justice for the oppressed;**
[right side] **who gives food to the hungry.**

The Lord sets the prisoners free;
God opens the eyes of the blind.

[left side] **God lifts up those who are bowed down;**
[right side] **God loves the righteous.**

The Lord watches over the strangers
and upholds the orphan and the widow,
but the way of the wicked comes to ruin.

[all] **God will reign forever,
for all generations.
Praise the Lord!**

God of joy,
each week we come ever closer to you.
We feel our hearts quickening with excitement
at the approach of Jesus' birth.
May our souls magnify you, as Mary's did.
May our lives point to yours, as John's did.
May we remain patient,
listening for your Word and your Spirit,
even as we prepare for the Christmas celebration.
With hope, peace, joy, and love we pray. **Amen.**

INVITATION TO DISCIPLESHIP

The invitation to discipleship may be led from the baptismal font.

It is the third week of Advent,
and we are getting used to waiting.
We wait to celebrate the one who has come.
We wait to meet the one who is still to come.
We wait to encounter the one who is always coming.
We wait with joy, but we do not wait idly.

As we wait, I invite you
to declare your trust and hope
in the one who has come,
is still coming,
and is always coming.
You may declare it with your mouth.
You may declare it with your hands and feet.
You may declare it with your mind and heart.
This week, let us strengthen our hearts
and make our declaration of faith.

PRAYERS OF INTERCESSION

The prayers of intercession may be led from the midst of the congregation.

God of wonders both told and untold,
through your holy word
we see images of the way the world could be.

The prophet Isaiah says,
"The wilderness and the dry land shall be glad,
the desert shall rejoice and blossom;
like the crocus it shall blossom abundantly,
and rejoice with joy and singing."
In the face of fire and drought,
of hurricanes and tornadoes,
as the climate changes more rapidly
than plants and animals can withstand,
give us strength to make changes of our own.
May we learn to consume only what we need
and take responsibility for the energy we use,
asking corporations and governments to do the same.

The prophet Isaiah says,
"They shall see the glory of God."
And we cry, "O Lord, let us see it."
Isaiah says, "The eyes of the blind shall be opened."
God, may it be so for us all.
Isaiah says, "The ears of the deaf shall be unstopped."
Help each of us to hear you more clearly.
Isaiah says, "The lame shall leap like a deer"
and "The tongue of the speechless shall sing for joy."
May our spirits leap together
and our voices rise to offer you praise.

The prophet Isaiah says:
"A highway shall be in the desert,
and it shall be called the Holy Way."
This Holy Way will connect us
to the north and south, the east and west.
We pray for people to our north . . .
We pray for people to our south . . .
We pray for people to our east . . .
We pray for people to our west . . .
For all of them and for all of us,
may we obtain joy and gladness.
May sorrow and sighing flee away.

May we be part of creating
this world Isaiah describes—
the world as it could be,
the world as it should be.
In Jesus' name we pray. **Amen.**

INVITATION TO OFFERING

The invitation to offering may be led from the Communion table.

May the joy we celebrate on this day
help us to remember our many blessings.
From that rich store, let us give back to God
a portion of what we have been given.

INVITATION TO THE TABLE

The invitation to the table is led from the Communion table.

We come to this table at God's invitation.
God has promised to fill us
with the good things at this table—
the bread and cup we share.

But God will also fill us
with hope and justice.
God will also fill us
with peace and connection.
God will also fill us
with joy, unity, and love.

CHARGE

The blessing and charge may be led from the doors of the church.

Be patient, beloved,
until the coming of God.
Strengthen your hearts,
for the time is drawing near.
Look for liberation,
and there you will glimpse God.
Amen. *or* **Thanks be to God.**

Fourth Sunday of Advent

Isaiah 7:10–16
Psalm 80:1–7, 17–19

Romans 1:1–7
Matthew 1:18–25

OPENING SENTENCES

The time is coming.
Indeed, it is almost here.

Restore us, God of hosts.
Let your face shine upon us, Emmanuel.

PRAYER OF THE DAY

Shepherd of Israel,
today we enter the last week of Advent,
this final time of waiting and preparation.
Do we have all the gifts?
No, because you are the gift we await.
Are all the lights up?
No, because the light of the world is still on the way.
Is our home ready for visitors?
Only if our home is ready for your arrival, O God.
And even as we wait for you to come,
we know that you are always with us—Emmanuel.
With hope, peace, joy, and love we pray. **Amen.**

---

*All this took place to fulfill what had been spoken by the
Lord through the prophet: "Look, the virgin shall conceive
and bear a son, and they shall name him Emmanuel," which
means, "God is with us."*

Matthew 1:22–23

INVITATION TO DISCIPLESHIP

The invitation to discipleship may be led from the baptismal font.

Joseph was about to dismiss Mary—
for righteousness' sake.
But the angel of God saw his righteousness
for what it really was—fear.

In this last week of Advent,
take inventory of your fears.
As you reflect on your fears,
remember that God is with you.
God will never turn away.
How might that promise transform your fear,
just as it did for Joseph?

PRAYERS OF INTERCESSION

The prayers of intercession may be led from the midst of the congregation.

God of angels and dreams,
God of Mary and Joseph,
in the midst of all our fears
we remember: **You are with us.**

God, sometimes we are afraid
of things happening in the world around us—
high unemployment rates,
warm winters and even warmer summers,
boarded-up buildings,
angry protestors,
nuclear weapons tests,
political grandstanding.
In the midst of all our fears
we remember: **You are with us.**

God, sometimes we are afraid
of things happening in the world within us—
depression, anxiety, mistrust,
jealousy, anger, and uncertainty.
In the midst of all our fears
we remember: **You are with us.**

God, sometimes we are afraid
of changes that shake our understanding
of how the world works,
and sometimes we are afraid
that the world will never change.
In the midst of all our fears
we remember: **You are with us.**

Sometimes we are afraid
that we will be overwhelmed
by the concerns of our hearts,
so we bring them now to you . . .
In the midst of all our fears
we remember: **You are with us.**

Sometimes we are afraid
that our joys will be drowned out,
so we lift them up now . . .
In the midst of all our joys
we remember: **You are with us.**

An angel of God tells Joseph not to be afraid,
and another angel says the same to Mary.
A host of angels exclaim
that the shepherds have nothing to fear,
all because you are there.
You are still here,
even as you are coming,
and through it all
we remember: **You are with us. Amen.**

INVITATION TO OFFERING

The invitation to offering may be led from the Communion table.

The greatest gift is on its way.
May we respond to that gift
with our own gifts,
offering our lives to the Lord.

INVITATION TO THE TABLE

The invitation to the table is led from the Communion table.

This is a table of love, not of fear,
but you don't have to be fearless to come here.
This is a table of joy, not of sadness,
but you don't have to be joyful to come here.
This is a table of peace, not of anger,
but you don't have to feel at peace to come here.
This is a table of hope, not of despair,
but you don't have to be hopeful to come here.

All are welcome at this table.
You are welcome at this table.
God is with us at this table.

CHARGE

The blessing and charge may be led from the doors of the church.

Friends, go out into the world and do not be afraid.
Turn to your neighbor and say, "God is with you!"
Turn to another neighbor and say, "God is with you!"
God is with you.
Amen. *or* **Thanks be to God.**

SEASON OF CHRISTMAS

Making Connections

The season of Christmas comprises the time from the Nativity of the Lord (December 25) to the Epiphany of the Lord (January 6). In this twelve-day celebration, the church rejoices at the birth of Jesus the Messiah and wonders at the mystery of the incarnation: "God with us" (Emmanuel) in human form. The Christmas season closes with an "epiphany" (meaning "manifestation" or "revelation")—that Jesus has come to bring good news not only to the people of Israel but to all the peoples of the earth. This is a particular point of concern in the Gospel of Matthew, the only evangelist to share the story of foreign sages paying homage with their gifts of gold, frankincense, and myrrh.

Indeed, in its account of the nativity of Jesus, Matthew's Gospel includes several scenes not featured in other accounts of the life of Christ. These include the visit of the magi (Matt. 2:1–12), the exodus to Egypt (Matt. 2:13–15), Herod's massacre of infants (Matt. 2:16–18), and the return of the Holy Family to Nazareth in Galilee (Matt. 2:19–23). These stories are connected with the Gospel of Matthew's context of Jewish Christianity and its presentation of Jesus as the "new Moses" sent to deliver the people of God from captivity to freedom.

Biblical scholars point out that the Gospel of Matthew is structured in such way as to mirror the five books of the Torah, or Pentateuch (Genesis, Exodus, Leviticus, Numbers, and Deuteronomy). After a prologue on the nativity of Jesus (Matt. 1:1–2:23), featured prominently during the season of Christmas in the Revised Common Lectionary, Matthew's Gospel consists of five distinct parts: (1) proclaiming God's realm (Matt. 3:1–7:29), (2) Jesus' ministry in Galilee (Matt. 8:1–11:1), (3) controversies and parables (Matt. 11:2–13:53), (4) the formation of the disciples (Matt. 13:54–19:2), and (5) the journey to Jerusalem (Matt. 19:3–25:46). Each of these five sections is further divided into two parts: Jesus' ministry and Jesus' teaching. The Gospel of Matthew concludes with the narrative of Jesus' death and resurrection (Matt. 26:1–28:20).

Year A of the Revised Common Lectionary offers us a chance to reflect on the Epiphany of the Lord and its related Gospel reading in the larger context of Matthew's story. As you prepare for the Christmas season, remember that the narrative of the Nativity is going somewhere: going forth with good news for all. Christmas is an opportunity to refocus the church's efforts around evangelism and outreach. The Christmas season (particularly the First Sunday in Year A) can also be a time to make connections with the contemporary experiences of immigrants and refugees, or children in danger. As worshipers contemplate New Year's resolutions, a commendable spiritual discipline might be a monthly reading of the Gospel of Matthew, one chapter a day.

The Christmas season can be an overwhelming time. May you be, like the magi, "overwhelmed with joy" (Matt. 2:10). And may that joy strengthen you to share the good news of the gospel: the epiphany of Emmanuel.

Seasonal/Repeating Resources

These resources are intended for regular use throughout the season of Christmas.

CONFESSION AND PARDON

The confession and pardon may be led from the baptismal font.

> Once we knew only the shadows;
> now we know the glory of God.
> Once we lived in deep despair;
> now the love of God shines upon us.
>
> Trusting in God's grace,
> let us confess our sin.

The confession may begin with a time of silence for personal prayer.

> **O Lord our God, we confess**
> **that we still stumble in the shadows.**
> **We are captive to our desires**
> **and limit those who long for freedom.**
> **We indulge in our weaknesses**
> **and use our strength to hurt others.**
>
> **Forgive us, O Lord our God.**
> **Break the yoke of oppression,**
> **and destroy the weapons of war.**
> **Set us free to serve you,**
> **and fill us with your peace.**
> **Establish your holy realm**
> **of justice and righteousness,**
> **now and forevermore;**
> **through Jesus Christ our Savior.**

Water may be poured or lifted from the baptismal font.

> A child has been born for us
> with the power and authority
> to set us free from sin forever.
> This child will be called
> wonderful and mighty,
> everlasting gift of peace.

> Believe the good news:
> In the name of Jesus Christ, we are forgiven.
> **Thanks be to God.**

PRAYER FOR ILLUMINATION

The prayer for illumination is led from the lectern or pulpit.

> God of beauty, goodness, and truth,
> guide the feet of the messenger
> who announces peace,
> who brings good news,
> who proclaims salvation.
> Fill us with your Holy Spirit,
> that we may break forth in singing,
> until all the ends of the earth
> echo the wonder of your work;
> through Jesus Christ our Lord. **Amen.**

THANKSGIVING FOR BAPTISM

The thanksgiving for baptism is led from the baptismal font.

The introductory dialogue ("The Lord be with you . . .") may be sung or spoken.

> To you, O Lord, we sing
> a new song of thanksgiving,
> rejoicing in the gift of baptism.
> In your goodness and kindness
> you have come to save us—
> not because of our works
> but because of your mercy,
> through the water of renewal
> and rebirth by your Holy Spirit.

Now with the rolling seas
we roar our "alleluias."
Now with the surging floods
we clap our hands in praise.
Now with all the earth
we sing of your steadfast love;
through Jesus Christ our Savior. **Amen.**

GREAT THANKSGIVING

The Great Thanksgiving is led from the Communion table.

The introductory dialogue ("The Lord be with you . . .") may be sung or spoken.

We praise you, O Lord,
for the gift of your Word.
From the very beginning,
your Word has been with you—
bringing all things into being,
giving life to all people.
Your Word came into the world
that all might believe.
Those who receive your Word
you claim as beloved children.

The Sanctus ("Holy, holy, holy . . .") may be sung or spoken.

We give you thanks, O Lord,
that in the fullness of time,
your Word became flesh
and came to live among us.
Now we have seen the glory
of your only begotten one.
Now we know the fullness
of your grace and truth.

The words of institution are included here, if not elsewhere, while the bread and cup are lifted (but not broken/poured).

Taking your Word upon our lips,
we promise ourselves to you.
From this fullness, let us all receive
grace upon grace upon grace.

A memorial acclamation ("Christ has died . . .") may be sung or spoken.

> We glorify you, O Lord,
> for the power of your Holy Spirit—
> the light that cannot be extinguished,
> the fire that will never go out.
> Send down your Spirit upon us
> and upon this bread and cup,
> that our hearts may burn within us
> as we share this meal in Jesus' name.
> Send us forth from this place
> to bring good news to the world,
> proclaiming your Word to all.

A Trinitarian doxology and Great Amen may be sung or spoken.

PRAYER AFTER COMMUNION

The prayer after Communion is led from the Communion table.

> Gracious God,
> you have gathered us here
> in the great company of your people
> to sing hymns of praise,
> hear the message of redemption,
> and share the feast of grace.
> Now send us out with songs of joy,
> that all the world may know
> the good news of salvation;
> through Jesus Christ our Lord. **Amen.**

PRAYER OF THANKSGIVING

The prayer of thanksgiving may be led from the Communion table.

We bless you, O Lord our God,
for you have blessed us
with every spiritual blessing—
the redemption of our souls,
the forgiveness of our sins,
the riches of your grace,
lovingly lavished upon us.
Gather up the gifts of our lives
and use them, in your wisdom,
to fulfill your good purpose.
Mark us with your Word
and seal us with your Spirit,
that we may praise your glory
now and in the world to come;
through Jesus Christ our Lord. **Amen.**

BLESSING

The blessing and charge may be led from the doors of the church.

May the great favor of God,
the gracious deeds of the Lord,
and the wondrous work of the Spirit
be with you now and always. **Alleluia!**

Christmas Eve/Nativity of the Lord, Proper I

December 24

Isaiah 9:2–7
Psalm 96

Titus 2:11–14
Luke 2:1–14 (15–20)

OPENING SENTENCES

The heavens and the earth are rejoicing.
¡Que cante a Dios toda la creación!
Let all creation sing to God!

Let the seas roar and the trees of the forest sing.
¡Que cante a Dios toda la creación!
Let all creation sing to God!

For the grace of God has appeared,
bringing salvation to all.
Cantemos a Dios una nueva cancion.
Let us sing to God a new song.
¡Que cante a Dios toda la creación!
Let all creation sing to God!

PRAYER OF THE DAY

On this day,
gratitude overflows from our hopeful hearts,
for the yoke of our burden,
the bar across our shoulders,
the rod of our oppressor
have been shattered—
through peace,
through justice,
through righteousness,
through a child. **Amen.**

INVITATION TO DISCIPLESHIP

The invitation to discipleship may be led from the baptismal font.

Good news is often scary.
There is risk in change.
The shepherds were terrified
when they saw an angel appear,
but he assured them there was nothing to fear.
So when the angel left,
the shepherds got up and went to witness
the good news of salvation.

Do not be afraid to find God
in the unexpected, in the vulnerable,
for God is with you.

PRAYERS OF INTERCESSION

The prayers of intercession may be led from the midst of the congregation.

You are grace incarnate, O God.
We come with joy and gratitude,
with songs of praise,
for you brought salvation to all.

On this day
we ask that you make us signs of your salvation
in the way we treat creation:
what we eat,
what we buy,
what we throw away.
Help us be your light, O God!

Make us signs of your salvation
in the way we treat each other:
whom we serve,
whom we listen to,
whom we include.
Help us be your light, O God!

Make us signs of your salvation
in the way we live our lives:
when we pray,
when we rest,
when we act.
Help us be your light, O God! Amen.

INVITATION TO OFFERING

The invitation to offering may be led from the Communion table.

Give to God, all families of the nations—
give to God glory and power!
Bring gifts!
For God is coming
to establish justice on the earth!

Let us bring our gifts to God,
joining the joyful song of creation.

INVITATION TO THE TABLE

The invitation to the table is led from the Communion table.

Set the table of grace,
bring additional chairs,
and make a bountiful meal—
for angels and shepherds,
entire oceans and forests,
and everything that lives in them
are coming to celebrate
the arrival of the Prince of Peace.

CHARGE

The blessing and charge may be led from the doors of the church.

Go and sing to God.
Declare the glory of the Wonderful Counselor,
and tell everyone that God's salvation is here!
Amen. *or* **Thanks be to God.**

Christmas Day/Nativity of the Lord, Proper II

December 25

Isaiah 62:6–12 Titus 3:4–7
Psalm 97 Luke 2:(1–7) 8–20

OPENING SENTENCES

> The angel has announced it:
> **Jesus, our Savior, is born!**
>
> Like the shepherds,
> let us share the good news:
> **Jesus, our Savior, is born!**
>
> Like the angels,
> let us praise God, saying:
> **Jesus, our Savior, is born!**
> **Glory to God in heaven**
> **and on earth peace**
> **among those whom God favors!**

PRAYER OF THE DAY

> God of glory,
> your goodness and loving-kindness
> have come to dwell among us,
> and salvation has knocked on our door.
> We can't wait to tell the world
> about this child,
> this joy we can't contain,
> this hope that came alive.
> Open our mouths
> and stretch out our arms,
> so we may sing your praises
> and embrace the child in a manger. **Amen.**

INVITATION TO DISCIPLESHIP

The invitation to discipleship may be led from the baptismal font.

Go through the gates
and prepare the way for the people!
Build the road;
clear away the stones!
For God's reign has begun;
justice and righteousness are its foundation,
and we are invited to be part of it.

We will be called holy people,
redeemed by the Lord.

PRAYERS OF INTERCESSION

The prayers of intercession may be led from the midst of the congregation.

Holy God,
we pray today for courage—
to make space for you
in the places that feel full,
where we say there is no place for you:
in our busy schedules,
in the tight deadlines,
in the ladder of success.
Child in the manger,
we welcome you.

We pray today for compassion—
to open ourselves
to the unexpected:
to traveling families,
to vulnerable children,
to humble gifts.
Child in the manger,
we welcome you.

We pray today for faith—
to believe in miracles:
an army of singing angels,
a world upside down,
God among us.
Child in the manger,
we welcome you. Amen.

INVITATION TO OFFERING

The invitation to offering may be led from the Communion table.

Through Jesus Christ,
God has poured the Holy Spirit on us.
Through the water of rebirth and renewal,
we have been saved,
not because of any works
of righteousness we have done,
but out of pure love.
Let us respond to this love
by offering our hearts and lives to God.

INVITATION TO THE TABLE

The invitation to the table is led from the Communion table.

The shepherds left everything behind
to see the one who came
to break bread with the world.
Let us come to the table, quickly,
and follow the song of the angels—
to break bread
and become bread:
whole loaves,
scattered crumbs,
feeding the world.

CHARGE

The blessing and charge may be led from the doors of the church.

Go through the gates;
prepare the way for the people!
Our deliverer has arrived!
Amen. *or* **Thanks be to God.**

Christmas Day/Nativity of the Lord, Proper III

December 25

Isaiah 52:7–10   Hebrews 1:1–4 (5–12)
Psalm 98   John 1:1–14

OPENING SENTENCES

How fast the world changes,
but your steadfast love is the same!

Everything seems uncertain,
but your faithfulness is the same!

In a world where nothing is permanent,
we give thanks—
for everything will perish,
but you remain.
You are the same,
and your years will never end.
Alleluia!

PRAYER OF THE DAY

Long ago you spoke to our ancestors
in many and various ways.
And then you came—
Word made flesh,
speaking new life,
sparking new light.
And you lived among us—
human, vulnerable,
divine, mighty,
complex as all of us.
We are witnesses of this miracle.
Bless our feet
as we announce your message. **Amen.**

The invitation to discipleship may be led from the baptismal font.

God is calling us today:
to break forth into joyous song,
to sing praises with the lyre,
to blow trumpets and horns,
to announce the good news of Christ's birth.

Come and sing a new song.
Christ is here.

PRAYERS OF INTERCESSION

The prayers of intercession may be led from the midst of the congregation.

Through you, light of all people,
all things came into being.
Everything you touched
came alive.

We pray today
for your creation:
for roaring seas,
for singing hills
and clapping floods.
**You became flesh
and made a home among us.**

We pray for the world
and those who live in it:
small birds and blue whales,
fungi and bacteria,
palm trees and pine trees,
bees and pollen.
**You became flesh
and made a home among us.**

We pray for your people:
young kids,
businesspeople,
artists, scientists,
wanderers, and doubters.
**You became flesh
and made a home among us.**

We pray for those
who laugh like you laughed,
who suffer like you suffered,
who love like you loved,
and we trust that you understand
their giggles, their tears, and their sighs.
You became flesh
and made a home among us. Amen.

INVITATION TO OFFERING

The invitation to offering may be led from the Communion table.

Everything came into being
through the Word made flesh.
Every blessing, every gift.

Let us bring forth our blessings and gifts,
for we have seen God's glory.

INVITATION TO THE TABLE

The invitation to the table is led from the Communion table.

Come to the feast
of the one who always remains,
for the heavens are the work of God's hands.
Come and enjoy a taste of eternity—
in this bread, in this wine,
the work of our hands,
so fleeting,
and so full of God's steadfast love.

CHARGE

The blessing and charge may be led from the doors of the church.

Now go and lift your voices.
Break forth together into singing.
Bring the good news,
announcing God's salvation.
Our God reigns!
Amen. *or* **Thanks be to God.**

First Sunday after Christmas Day

December 26–January 1

Isaiah 63:7–9   Hebrews 2:10–18
Psalm 148   Matthew 2:13–23

OPENING SENTENCES

God spoke,
and the sun, and the moon,
and bright stars were created.
Praise God from heaven,
praise God in the heights!

God spoke
and gave breath
to all the people and rulers of the earth.
Praise God from heaven,
praise God in the heights!

God spoke
and strengthened the people,
opening the gates of freedom.
Praise God from heaven,
praise God in the heights!

PRAYER OF THE DAY

Maker of the universe,
all creation sings your praise,
for all things exist for you
and through you.
We come to you this day
with our joys and sorrows,
our victories and struggles,
our minds and souls,
our flesh and bones,
with everything we are.
We sing to you this day,
joining the whispering winds
and the clapping leaves
in their song of love. **Amen.**

INVITATION TO DISCIPLESHIP

The invitation to discipleship may be led from the baptismal font.

Friends, do not be ashamed
to proclaim God's name to your siblings,
for it is clear that Jesus did not come
to help angels, but us,
the descendants of God's promise.

PRAYERS OF INTERCESSION

The prayers of intercession may be led from the midst of the congregation.

Holy One,
you know the pain of your people.
Escucha nuestras plegarias.
Listen to our prayers.

We pray for desperate parents
who have to leave their land
to ensure the survival of their children.
Escucha nuestras plegarias.
Listen to our prayers.

We pray for families
traveling from country to country
in search of a future without violence.
Escucha nuestras plegarias.
Listen to our prayers.

We pray for hospitable people
who open their hearts and homes
to weary travelers.
Escucha nuestras plegarias.
Listen to our prayers.

We pray for peace and flourishing
so that no one
will ever have to leave their home again.
Escucha nuestras plegarias.
Listen to our prayers. Amen.

INVITATION TO OFFERING

The invitation to offering may be led from the Communion table.

Let us remember God's faithful acts
and sing God's praises
because of all God has done for us.
God has treated us with compassion
and with deep affection.

Let us remember and give generously
by offering our songs, our prayers, and our lives.

INVITATION TO THE TABLE

The invitation to the table is led from the Communion table.

"Surely, they are my people,"
says our God—
setting the table,
making space for us,
according to his mercy,
according to the abundance of her steadfast love.

Surely, we are God's people.
Let us join the feast.

CHARGE

The blessing and charge may be led from the doors of the church.

During all our distress,
God also was distressed.
So God sent a messenger to save us.
Go and be God's messenger
to our hurting world.
Amen. *or* **Thanks be to God.**

Second Sunday after Christmas Day

January 2–5

Jeremiah 31:7–14 *or*
  Sirach 24:1–12
Psalm 147:12–20 *or*
  Wisdom 10:15–21

Ephesians 1:3–14
John 1:(1–9) 10–18

OPENING SENTENCES

Sing aloud with gladness to our gathering God,
who draws us in from far and near.

Be radiant over the goodness of the Lord.
Come, rejoice in the dance.

PRAYER OF THE DAY

God of abundance,
you graciously provide for all your children.
Open our hearts, our hands, and our homes
to all of your creation, our adopted family,
bound together not by biology or marriage,
location or government,
but by the richness of your grace in Jesus Christ,
sealed with the promise of your Holy Spirit,
who intercedes for us with sighs too deep for words,
and in whose power we pray. **Amen.**

INVITATION TO DISCIPLESHIP

The invitation to discipleship may be led from the baptismal font.

God has chosen us as beloved children
to receive the abundance of divine grace,
to dwell in the presence of the one who created us and knows us.

How will you live as a child of God this week?
Knowing that God extends the same abundant grace
to everyone around you,
how might you treat them?

PRAYERS OF INTERCESSION

The prayers of intercession may be led from the midst of the congregation.

We give you thanks, O God, for calling us your children.
In solidarity with our siblings across your creation,
we cry out:
"Save, O Lord, your people!"
Lord, in your mercy, **hear our prayer.**

We pray for your creation . . .
May this earth, our home,
Brother Moon and Sister Sun,
the grass, the trees, the water, the sky,
be sustained by your command and preserved from our greed.
Lord, in your mercy, **hear our prayer.**

We pray for your human family . . .
May we stop fighting and seek peace,
walking in the path of your *shalom*,
in which we shall not stumble.
Lord, in your mercy, **hear our prayer.**

We pray for your church . . .
May it be what you have called it to be:
a refuge for the poor,
a home for the displaced and the forgotten,
a house not of scarcity but of abundance.
Lord, in your mercy, **hear our prayer.**

We pray for loved ones . . .
Turn their mourning into joy,
give them gladness for sorrow,
teach us how to comfort them, even as you comfort us.
Lord, in your mercy, **hear our prayer.**

O God, may we be satisfied
by what we receive from your hands,
even as we long for the fullness of your grace
to redeem and restore your fractured family;
through Jesus Christ our Lord,
in the power of your Holy Spirit. **Amen.**

INVITATION TO OFFERING

The invitation to offering may be led from the Communion table.

Let us return our gifts to God
from the bounty bestowed upon us.
Like watered gardens, may we bear fruit
for the good of all God's creation.

Let us offer our whole selves to our God.

INVITATION TO THE TABLE

The invitation to the table is led from the Communion table.

Come, be radiant over God's goodness,
over the grain, the wine, and the oil.
Be satisfied with God's bounty.
This is the table of God's rich grace,
prepared for all who would receive it.

CHARGE

The blessing and charge may be led from the doors of the church.

Live for the praise of God's glory.
Live as beloved children of a generous God.
Amen. *or* **Thanks be to God.**

Epiphany of the Lord

January 6 (or previous Sunday)

Isaiah 60:1–6   Ephesians 3:1–12
Psalm 72:1–7, 10–14   Matthew 2:1–12

OPENING SENTENCES

Arise, shine, for your light has come,
and the glory of the Lord has risen upon you.

Come, see and be radiant.
Come, thrill and rejoice.

PRAYER OF THE DAY

God of the sunrise and the evening star,
you have revealed to us your love in Jesus Christ:
a love so long expected
yet so surprising in its unfolding.
Gather us from near and far.
Awaken us to your unexpected revelation,
the justice of your slow-dawning kin-dom,
the mystery of your boundless invitation.
Shine through us,
that all people would be drawn to your light in us;
through Jesus Christ,
in whom we have access to you in boldness
and confidence through faith to pray. **Amen.**

---

*May the kings of Tarshish and of the isles render him tribute,
may the kings of Sheba and Seba bring gifts. May all kings
fall down before him, all nations give him service. For he
delivers the needy when they call, the poor and those who
have no helper.*

Psalm 72:10–12

INVITATION TO DISCIPLESHIP

The invitation to discipleship may be led from the baptismal font.

God calls us all, from near and from far,
from unanticipated corners of this wide world,
to bear witness to the dawning revelation
of divine love in Jesus Christ.

In what unexpected ways have you seen God at work,
and how might you join that work?
How will you reflect God's radiant love?

PRAYERS OF INTERCESSION

The prayers of intercession may be led from the midst of the congregation.

Righteous God, you deliver the needy when they call.
Hear now our prayers for your people and your creation.

For all who seek the brightness of your love,
whether they share our religious tradition or not,
may they lift their eyes, see that love, and rejoice.

For all who look for the dawn of justice,
may they find your deliverance close at hand.

For all who gaze unflinchingly
into the night sky of our humanity—
illness and disease, violence and oppression—
hoping to see the first star of healing and wholeness,
may they glimpse your coming redemption.

For your creation,
which waits with eager longing for your revelation,
for freedom from its bondage to decay,
may your radiance water the earth like a spring shower.

O God, in these days
may righteousness flourish and peace abound,
as long as the sun and moon endure,
throughout all generations. **Amen.**

INVITATION TO OFFERING

The invitation to offering may be led from the Communion table.

As the magi brought gifts
to pay homage to the one born King,
so let us bring our gifts
to proclaim the praise of our God.

INVITATION TO THE TABLE

The invitation to the table is led from the Communion table.

The mountains have yielded their prosperity
at the coming of the one who falls like rain on mown grass.
God has provided that abundance at this table,
an abundance of nourishment and of grace.

This is God's table, and God welcomes all,
even those we might not anticipate,
even those who might not expect the invitation.

CHARGE

The blessing and charge may be led from the doors of the church.

Reflect the warm brilliance of God's love,
even as you seek the dawn in unexpected places.
Amen. *or* **Thanks be to God.**

TIME AFTER THE EPIPHANY

Making Connections

The Time after the Epiphany (also called "Ordinary Time") refers to the span of Sundays between the seasons of Christmas and Lent, bracketed by the Baptism and Transfiguration of the Lord. The length of this period varies from six to nine weeks depending on the date of Easter. There is not an overarching theological theme or liturgical focus for the Time after the Epiphany, as there is with the seasons of Advent, Christmas, Lent, and Easter. Rather, this time in the Christian year is characterized by a weekly rhythm—the church's witness to the resurrection on the Lord's Day. It is about keeping those Sundays and proclaiming the gospel "in order."

At the heart of the Time after the Epiphany in Revised Common Lectionary Year A is one of the most well-known and well-loved passages of Christian Scripture: the Sermon on the Mount (Matt. 5:1–7:29). The early church leader Augustine (354–430) considered this discourse of Jesus to be a perfect summary of Christian life. In contemporary times it has inspired the ethics and activism of Leo Tolstoy, Mahatma Gandhi, Dietrich Bonhoeffer, and Martin Luther King Jr.

Beginning with the Beatitudes (Matt. 5:3–12), the Sermon on the Mount includes Jesus' metaphors of the church as salt and light (Matt. 5:13–16); his interpretation of the Ten Commandments (Matt. 5:17–37); the calling to love one's enemies (Matt. 5:38–48); guidance on almsgiving, fasting, and prayer (Matt. 6:1–18), including the Lord's Prayer (Matt. 6:9–13); sayings on stewardship and providence (Matt. 6:19–34); and other wisdom for the church, including teachings on judgment (Matt. 7:1–5), the injunction to "ask, search, and knock" (Matt. 7:7–11), the Golden Rule (Matt. 7:12), the narrow gate (Matt. 7:13–14), a warning about false prophets (Matt. 7:15–20), and the illustration of houses built on rock or sand (Matt. 7:24–27). Many of these passages are included in the Gospel readings for the Time after the Epiphany in Year A, although worshipers will hear more of the Sermon on the Mount when Easter arrives later. Readings from the Hebrew Scriptures provide context for Jesus' teaching through the words of the law and the prophets; selections from First Corinthians underscore the gifts and challenges of life in community.

The Time after the Epiphany provides an excellent occasion for focused reflection on the Sermon on the Mount, both within worship and beyond. Congregations might organize a public reading of the whole sermon, followed by a time for discussion and reflection. Small groups or committees of the church might wish to study it together, reflecting on its implications for their ministry and mission. Individuals might choose to read portions of the sermon in personal devotion. In these and other ways, the Sermon on the Mount can become a call to action in Christian life and serve as a blueprint for building up the church. As Jesus says near the conclusion of the discourse: "Everyone then who hears these words of mine and acts on them will be like a wise [person] who built [a] house on rock" (Matt. 7:24).

These are no "ordinary" words. Let them speak to you anew in this Time after the Epiphany.

Seasonal/Repeating Resources

These resources are intended for regular use throughout the Time after the Epiphany.

CONFESSION AND PARDON

The confession and pardon may be led from the baptismal font.

People of God,
in the covenant of baptism
we are claimed in Christ Jesus
and called to be saints.

Therefore, with faith and confidence
let us confess our sin and ask for God's grace,
calling on the name of our Savior and Lord.

The confession may begin with a time of silence for personal prayer.

**Holy One, in your presence
we confess our captivity to sin
and our resistance to your way.
You have chosen what is foolish
to shame the wisdom of this world,
but we boast in our knowledge
and ignore the insights of others.
You have chosen what is weak
to shame the powers of this world,
but we boast in our strength
and refuse the gifts of others.
You have chosen what is despised
to shame the values of this world,
but we boast in our merits
and reject the worth of others.**

Forgive us, Holy One.
Renew and reshape our lives
with the message of the cross.
Teach us to boast in nothing
but the crucified and risen one:
Jesus Christ our Lord.

Water may be poured or lifted from the baptismal font.

Christ is the wisdom of God.
Christ is the power of God.
Christ is the glory of God.

In the name of Jesus Christ, we are forgiven.
Thanks be to God.

PRAYER FOR ILLUMINATION

The prayer for illumination is led from the lectern or pulpit.

Send your Spirit, O God,
to search us and teach us.
Help us to understand
the wisdom of your way.
Give us the mind of Christ—
by whose gracious word we live
and in whose holy name we pray. **Amen.**

THANKSGIVING FOR BAPTISM

The thanksgiving for baptism is led from the baptismal font.

*The introductory dialogue ("The Lord be with you . . .") may be sung or
spoken.*

O Holy One, our God, we praise you.
You created the heavens and shaped the earth.
You gave the breath of life to all creatures
and poured out your Spirit on all flesh.
We give thanks for the gift of baptism.
Here you claim us in your covenant.
Here you call us to lives of righteousness
and sign us with the glory of your name.
Continue to pour out your Spirit upon us.

Let us live as your faithful servants.
Let us teach others to walk in your paths
and establish justice throughout the earth.
All this we pray in the name of Jesus—
your chosen one, in whom you delight;
your beloved, in whom you are well pleased;
and our Savior and Lord. **Amen.**

GREAT THANKSGIVING

The Great Thanksgiving is led from the Communion table.

The introductory dialogue ("The Lord be with you . . .") may be sung or spoken.

Blessed are you, O God,
creator of heaven and earth.
From generation to generation
you have cared for your people.
You bless the poor in spirit
with the kingdom of heaven.
You bless those who mourn
with your comfort and peace.
You bless the meek and lowly
with the inheritance of the earth.
Therefore, with joy and gladness
we join with all the saints
in singing thanks and praise.

The Sanctus ("Holy, holy, holy . . .") may be sung or spoken.

Blessed are you, O God,
redeemer of the world.
Into this life of sin and sorrow
you sent Jesus Christ to save us.
He blesses those who hunger and thirst
with justice and righteousness.
He blesses those who are merciful
with your abundant mercy.
He blesses the pure in heart
with the revelation of your glory.

The words of institution are included here, if not elsewhere, while the bread and cup are lifted (but not broken/poured).

Therefore, with joy and gladness
we offer ourselves to you
as we share this sacred meal.

A memorial acclamation ("Christ has died . . .") may be sung or spoken.

Blessed are you, O God,
sustainer and source of all life.
On your people and in this meal
you pour out your Holy Spirit.
Now bless the peacemakers
with the name "children of God."
Now bless those who are persecuted
with the reward of the righteous.
Now bless all who suffer evil
with the welcome of your eternal realm.
Then with joy and gladness
we will glorify you together,
one God, forever and ever.

A Trinitarian doxology and Great Amen may be sung or spoken.

PRAYER AFTER COMMUNION

The prayer after Communion is led from the Communion table.

Gracious God, at this table
you have blessed us with your presence.
Now send us forth in your Spirit
to be a blessing in the world;
in the name of Jesus Christ our Lord. **Amen.**

PRAYER OF THANKSGIVING

The prayer of thanksgiving may be led from the Communion table.

What can we offer to you, O Lord,
as our sacrifice of thanks and praise?
You have shown us what is good
and the offering you require of us.
Help us to do justice, to love kindness,
and to walk humbly with you, our God;
in the name of Christ our Savior. **Amen.**

BLESSING

The blessing and charge may be led from the doors of the church.

Now the Son of God is rising,
the Spirit of God is descending,
and the voice of God is speaking:
"You are my beloved people;
with you I am well pleased." **Alleluia!**

Baptism of the Lord

January 7–13

Isaiah 42:1–9
Psalm 29

Acts 10:34–43
Matthew 3:13–17

OPENING SENTENCES

God says: "I am the Lord,
I have called you in righteousness;
I have taken you by the hand."
**God gives us as a covenant to the people,
a light to the nations.**

God says: "I am the Lord,
that is my name;
my glory I give to no other."
**The former things have come to pass;
now God declares a new thing.**

Let us worship God.

PRAYER OF THE DAY

Holy One, in the waters of the Jordan
you claimed Jesus as your beloved Son.
Send your Holy Spirit to anoint us,
that we may be filled with your grace
and live as your beloved children;
in the name of Jesus Christ our Lord. **Amen.**

INVITATION TO DISCIPLESHIP

The invitation to discipleship may be led from the baptismal font.

The call to discipleship begins with baptism.
If you are ready
to enter into the body of Christ
and the life of the church,
come to the waters—

come and be baptized,
claimed as Christ's own.
If you are ready
to renew your commitment
as a disciple of Jesus,
come to the waters—
come and reaffirm
the promise of your baptism.

Whoever you are,
wherever you come from,
Jesus is ready to meet you at the water.

PRAYERS OF INTERCESSION

The prayers of intercession may be led from the midst of the congregation.

O Lord our God,
give strength to your people,
and bless us with your peace.
Hear our prayer.

For those who have no peace . . .
Deliver them from danger.

For those who are oppressed . . .
Release them from their captivity.

For those who are treated unfairly . . .
Lift them up in your love.

For those who hunger and thirst . . .
Provide abundantly for them.

For those who need healing . . .
Surround them with your care.

For those who are despairing . . .
Send the message of good news.

O Lord our God,
give strength to your people,
and bless us with your peace;
in the name of Jesus Christ,
our Sovereign and Savior. **Amen.**

INVITATION TO OFFERING

The invitation to offering may be led from the Communion table.

The former things have come to pass,
and now new things are springing forth.

Let us share in the new thing God is doing
by offering our gifts and lives to the Lord.

INVITATION TO THE TABLE

The invitation to the table is led from the Communion table.

Jesus died on the cross,
but God raised him on the third day.
And we are witnesses—
we ate and drank with him
when he had risen from the dead.

Let us return to the table of grace
to eat and drink with Jesus,
the crucified and risen Lord.

CHARGE

The blessing and charge may be led from the doors of the church.

Go forth as a beloved child of God,
sharing Christ's message of peace.
Amen. *or* **Thanks be to God.**

Second Sunday after the Epiphany

January 14–20

Isaiah 49:1–7

Psalm 40:1–11

1 Corinthians 1:1–9

John 1:29–42

OPENING SENTENCES

Come and see what God has done.
Here is the Lamb of God,
who takes away the sin of the world.

Come and see what God has done.
We have found the Messiah,
the anointed one of God.

PRAYER OF THE DAY

Holy One,
you sent the Lord Jesus Christ
to save the world from sin.
Teach us to follow him faithfully,
proclaiming the good news,
that all may come to know
and love the Lamb of God,
in whose name we pray. **Amen.**

INVITATION TO DISCIPLESHIP

The invitation to discipleship may be led from the baptismal font.

When the first followers of Jesus
saw their teacher passing by,
they cried out, "Rabbi, where are you staying?"
Jesus responded, "Come and see."

Jesus makes the same invitation to you:
Come and see what God is doing now—
in your life, in this community of faith,
and in the world God loves so much.
Come and see.

PRAYERS OF INTERCESSION

The prayers of intercession may be led from the midst of the congregation.

We are waiting patiently for you, O Lord.
Come to us and hear our cry.
Out of the depths we lift up our prayers.

We pray for the church in all the world . . .
that we might offer new songs of praise
to share the new things you are doing.

We pray for the nations of the earth . . .
that they may put down the weapons of war
and take up the gospel of peace.

We pray for people who are in trouble . . .
that you would raise them up from the pit
and make their steps secure.

We pray for refugees and people in exile . . .
that they may have safe passage
and find shelter and welcome in the land.

We pray for those who are sick . . .
that they may know your saving power
and be delivered from their suffering.

We pray for new disciples of Jesus . . .
that you will nourish them in this fellowship
and keep them faithful in Christ's service.

Do not withhold your mercy, O Lord.
Let your steadfast love and faithfulness
keep us safe forever;
through Jesus Christ our Lord. **Amen.**

INVITATION TO OFFERING

The invitation to offering may be led from the Communion table.

We are not lacking in spiritual gifts.
God has supported and strengthened us
to carry out the work of the gospel.

With gratitude to God for the grace of Jesus Christ,
let us offer our gifts and our lives to the Lord.

INVITATION TO THE TABLE

The invitation to the table is led from the Communion table.

This is the supper of the Lamb of God,
who takes away the sin of the world.
Jesus is our host at this feast.

Come and share this holy meal.
Taste and see the goodness of the Lord.

CHARGE

The blessing and charge may be led from the doors of the church.

Jesus has invited us to "come and see"
the saving work of God in the world.
Now go and tell this good news to all.
Amen. *or* **Thanks be to God.**

Third Sunday after the Epiphany

January 21–27

Isaiah 9:1–4
Psalm 27:1, 4–9

1 Corinthians 1:10–18
Matthew 4:12–23

OPENING SENTENCES

The Lord is my light and salvation;
whom shall I fear?
**The Lord is the stronghold of my life;
of whom shall I be afraid?**

One thing I asked of the Lord,
that I will seek after:
**to live in the house of the Lord
all the days of my life.**

PRAYER OF THE DAY

Holy One,
you meet us where we are
and call us to step forth in faith.
Claim us as disciples,
and strengthen us by your Spirit
to follow you faithfully,
that we may share good news with all;
through Jesus Christ our Savior. **Amen.**

INVITATION TO DISCIPLESHIP

The invitation to discipleship may be led from the baptismal font.

As Jesus called to the fishers—
Peter, Andrew, James, and John—
Jesus calls to us today:
"Follow me,
and I will make you fish for people."

How will you answer this call?

PRAYERS OF INTERCESSION

The prayers of intercession may be led from the midst of the congregation.

Hear us, O Lord, when we cry aloud.
Be gracious to us and answer us!
God of grace, **hear our prayer.**

We pray for the church . . .
Give us peace and heal our divisions,
that we may be more faithful
in sharing the message of the cross.
God of grace, **hear our prayer.**

We pray for the earth . . .
Out of your great abundance
restore the beauty of creation,
and provide a plentiful harvest for all.
God of grace, **hear our prayer.**

We pray for all peoples . . .
Break the yokes of oppression,
relieve the burdens of injustice,
and set all captives free.
God of grace, **hear our prayer.**

We pray for this community . . .
Accompany us in our daily lives,
our work and rest and play,
as we seek to do your will.
God of grace, **hear our prayer.**

We pray for loved ones . . .
Shelter them in times of trouble,
and lift them up to places of safety,
that they may rejoice and sing your praise.
God of grace, **hear our prayer.**

It is your face, O Lord, that we seek.
Do not turn away from us,
for you are our help and salvation. **Amen.**

INVITATION TO OFFERING

The invitation to offering may be led from the Communion table.

Come before the God of glory,
bringing all that you have
and all that you are,
and God will multiply our gifts
and increase our joy.

Let us offer our lives to God
with gladness and praise.

INVITATION TO THE TABLE

The invitation to the table is led from the Communion table.

At this table we are made whole.
That which is broken will be mended,
and those who are divided will be reconciled,
as all are gathered into one body.

Come to this table
and know the healing, reconciling love of God
through Jesus Christ our Savior.

CHARGE

The blessing and charge may be led from the doors of the church.

Go forth as fishers of people,
proclaiming the good news of God's realm.
Amen. *or* **Thanks be to God.**

Fourth Sunday after the Epiphany

January 28–February 3

Micah 6:1–8   1 Corinthians 1:18–31
Psalm 15   Matthew 5:1–12

OPENING SENTENCES

O Lord, who may abide in your tent?
Who may dwell on your holy hill?

Those who walk blamelessly,
and do what is right,
and speak the truth from their heart.
**Those who do these things
shall never be moved.**

PRAYER OF THE DAY

Holy God,
you call unexpected disciples—
those who are poor and meek,
those who are hungry and thirsty,
those who are reviled and persecuted—
to be a blessing for the world.
Number us among those saints,
that we may serve your purpose
and share the blessing;
through Jesus Christ our Savior. **Amen.**

INVITATION TO DISCIPLESHIP

The invitation to discipleship may be led from the baptismal font.

Consider your calling.
God isn't looking for disciples
who are famous for their wisdom,
feared for their might,
or honored for their status.

God chooses the foolish,
the weak, and the despised—
that we might rejoice
in the wisdom, power, and glory
of Jesus Christ our Lord.

Consider your calling.
Come and join us in following Jesus.

PRAYERS OF INTERCESSION

The prayers of intercession may be led from the midst of the congregation.

O Lord our God,
we come into your presence
with prayers for the world you love.
God of grace, **hear our prayer.**

We pray for the church . . .
Give us your wisdom,
and uphold us with your strength
as we share the message of the cross.
God of grace, **hear our prayer.**

We pray for the earth . . .
Protect your creatures from destruction,
and purify the waters, air, and soil,
that all the earth may sing your praise.
God of grace, **hear our prayer.**

We pray for all peoples . . .
Dismantle systems of injustice,
and destroy weapons of violence,
that all may live in dignity and peace.
God of grace, **hear our prayer.**

We pray for this community . . .
Protect those who are persecuted,
and defend those who are reviled,
that they may receive their righteous reward.
God of grace, **hear our prayer.**

We pray for loved ones . . .
Support those who are suffering,
and comfort those who mourn
with the power of your Holy Spirit.
God of grace, **hear our prayer.**

You are the source of our life, O Lord.
Grant us wisdom, righteousness,
sanctification, and redemption.
This we pray in Jesus' name. **Amen.**

INVITATION TO OFFERING

The invitation to offering may be led from the Communion table.

What does the Lord require of us?
Burnt offerings or rivers of oil?
The fruit of our bodies for the sins of our souls?

No, God has shown us what is good.
With justice, kindness, and humility,
let us offer our lives to the Lord.

INVITATION TO THE TABLE

The invitation to the table is led from the Communion table.

The Lord Jesus Christ says:
"Blessed are those who hunger and thirst
for righteousness, for they will be filled."

This is the table of the Lord.
Bring your hunger, bring your thirst.
Come and taste the bread of life.
Come and share the cup of blessing.
Come and be filled with God's grace.

CHARGE

The blessing and charge may be led from the doors of the church.

Let us go forth from this place
doing justice, loving kindness,
and walking humbly with our God.
Amen. *or* **Thanks be to God.**

Fifth Sunday after the Epiphany

February 4–10

Isaiah 58:1–9a (9b–12)   1 Corinthians 2:1–12 (13–16)
Psalm 112:1–9 (10)   Matthew 5:13–20

OPENING SENTENCES

Praise the Lord!
Happy are those who worship the Lord,
who delight in God's commandments.

The righteous will never be moved;
they will be remembered forever.

PRAYER OF THE DAY

God of heaven and earth,
you sent Jesus into this world
not to abolish the law and prophets
but to fulfill them.
Fulfill your purpose in us,
that your will may be done
on earth as in heaven;
through Christ our Lord. **Amen.**

INVITATION TO DISCIPLESHIP

The invitation to discipleship may be led from the baptismal font.

Beloved, each one of us
has received gifts of the Spirit
for proclaiming the saving love of Christ
and the great mystery of God.
Through our words and actions,
our prayers and offerings,
our worship and service,
we are called to reveal
the reign of God on earth.

How will you fulfill this calling?
How will you join us in this work?
We welcome you in Christ's service.

PRAYERS OF INTERCESSION

The prayers of intercession may be led from the midst of the congregation.

We call on you, O Lord,
knowing that you will answer.
We cry to you for help,
waiting to hear you say: Here I am.
God of grace, **hear our prayer.**

We pray for the church . . .
Help us to be like salt of the earth
and light shining in the world,
that all may taste and see your goodness.
God of grace, **hear our prayer.**

We pray for the earth . . .
Restore the ruins of creation,
and provide water in parched places,
that all generations may know your glory.
God of grace, **hear our prayer.**

We pray for all peoples . . .
Help us to break the bonds of injustice
and let the oppressed go free,
for this is the service you desire.
God of grace, **hear our prayer.**

We pray for this community . . .
Give bread to those who are hungry
and shelter to those without houses,
that we may live as one human family.
God of grace, **hear our prayer.**

We pray for loved ones . . .
Strengthen weak hearts and bones,
and renew those who are weary
with the living water of your mercy.
God of grace, **hear our prayer.**

Holy One, our God,
let your light break forth like the dawn,
and let your healing power spring forth,
that we may know your saving work;
through Jesus Christ our Lord. **Amen.**

INVITATION TO OFFERING

The invitation to offering may be led from the Communion table.

Who are the righteous of the Lord?
They are gracious and merciful;
they deal generously with others
and conduct their affairs with justice;
they freely share what they have
and give to those who are in need.

Let us share in the work of the saints
by offering our gifts to God.

INVITATION TO THE TABLE

The invitation to the table is led from the Communion table.

This is the worship God chooses:
to share bread with those who are hungry,
to welcome those in need of shelter,
to clothe the vulnerable with care,
and to reconcile the human family.

This is the feast of salvation,
where the needs of the world are met
and the promises of God are fulfilled.

CHARGE

The blessing and charge may be led from the doors of the church.

Let your light shine before others,
that they may see works of goodness
and give glory to God.
Amen. *or* **Thanks be to God.**

Sixth Sunday after the Epiphany

February 11–17, if before the Transfiguration

Deuteronomy 30:15–20 1 Corinthians 3:1–9
  or Sirach 15:15–20 Matthew 5:21–37
Psalm 119:1–8

OPENING SENTENCES

Happy are those whose way is blameless,
who walk in the law of the Lord.
Happy are those who keep God's decrees,
who seek the Lord with their whole heart.

O that my ways may be steadfast
in keeping God's statutes!
Then I shall not be put to shame,
having my eyes fixed
on the commandments of the Lord.

PRAYER OF THE DAY

O Lord our God,
you have given us your law
to teach us how to live in peace,
to be faithful in our relationships,
and to be trustworthy in our words.
Help us to take the extra step
in rejecting violence,
loving our neighbors,
and speaking the truth,
that we may be reconciled to you
and to one another;
through Jesus Christ our Savior. **Amen.**

INVITATION TO DISCIPLESHIP

The invitation to discipleship may be led from the baptismal font.

If you have a seed of faith within you
and want to help it grow,
we welcome you.

If you are feeling burnt out and dried up,
in need of refreshment and renewal,
we welcome you.

We believe that God is already at work in you
and that you have a place and purpose here.

PRAYERS OF INTERCESSION

The prayers of intercession may be led from the midst of the congregation.

Great is your wisdom, O Lord;
you are mighty in power
and vigilant in your care.
Therefore we come to you in faith.
God of grace, **hear our prayer.**

We pray for the church . . .
Build us up as Christ's body,
and strengthen us to serve you.
God of grace, **hear our prayer.**

We pray for the earth . . .
Bring life out of death and destruction,
and bless your creation with renewal.
God of grace, **hear our prayer.**

We pray for all peoples . . .
Teach us to pursue peace
and work for reconciliation.
God of grace, **hear our prayer.**

We pray for this community . . .
Restore the honor of those falsely accused,
and be present with those who are in prison.
God of grace, **hear our prayer.**

We pray for loved ones . . .
Protect those who are sick or suffering,
in danger or facing death.
God of grace, **hear our prayer.**

Lead us, O Lord, through fire and flood.
Guide us, O God, from death to life.
This we pray in Jesus' name. **Amen.**

INVITATION TO OFFERING

The invitation to offering may be led from the Communion table.

We may plant the seeds or water the garden,
but it is God alone who gives the growth.
We are God's servants, working together
to sow seeds of peace on earth
and build up the body of Christ.

Trusting in what God is doing,
let us offer our gifts to the Lord.

INVITATION TO THE TABLE

The invitation to the table is led from the Communion table.

Like infants, Jesus feeds us with his body,
nourishing us and helping us to grow
until we are ready for the holy banquet
at the wedding feast of heaven and earth.

As children of God, come to the table.
Come and be strengthened
by the grace of the Lord Jesus Christ,
the love of God,
and the communion of the Holy Spirit.

CHARGE

The blessing and charge may be led from the doors of the church.

Each day we face choices
between life and death, blessing and curse.
Let us choose blessing and life,
that we may live and share God's blessing with all.
Amen. *or* **Thanks be to God.**

Seventh Sunday after the Epiphany

February 18–24, if before the Transfiguration

Leviticus 19:1–2, 9–18
Psalm 119:33–40

1 Corinthians 3:10–11, 16–23
Matthew 5:38–48

OPENING SENTENCES

Teach us, O Lord, the way of your statutes,
and we will observe it to the end.
Give us understanding,
that we may keep your law
and observe it with our whole hearts.

Lead us in the path of your commandments,
for we delight in that path.
Turn our hearts to your decrees
and not to selfish gain.
Turn our eyes from looking at vanities;
give us life in your ways.

PRAYER OF THE DAY

Holy One,
you call us to live our lives as builders
on the framework of justice and mercy
you have constructed.
Lead us not to build monuments to human vanity,
but structures of care, compassion, and justice
for the world you created in beauty and love.
Guide us this day
so we may build a house where all are welcome. **Amen.**

"You shall not take vengeance or bear a grudge against any
of your people, but you shall love your neighbors as yourself:
I am the LORD."

Leviticus 19:18

INVITATION TO DISCIPLESHIP

The invitation to discipleship may be led from the baptismal font.

If you've been searching for a faith community
where you can join with others to work for God's vision,
there is room for you here.
God calls us to build a better world,
and we seek to live into God's dream for us.

Come join us.

PRAYERS OF INTERCESSION

The prayers of intercession may be led from the midst of the congregation.

Holy One,
you have laid for us a foundation in Christ Jesus,
and you invite us to participate in the work
of building on that foundation.
We may not reach the ending,
but as laborers in your crew, we can start,
slowly, but surely, mending—
brick by brick, heart by heart.
Show us your way.
Teach us your precepts,
that we may build on a solid foundation.

We pray for the church.
May we be a sign that points to you
rather than to our own image.
May we be places and communities of justice
where people are fed to go and feed others.
Lord, in your mercy, **hear our prayer.**

We pray for the world.
Lead us into your abundance,
that we may share with gratitude,
feed others without resentment,
and trust in your goodness for all.
Lord, in your mercy, **hear our prayer.**

We pray for this community.
Expand our understanding
of who you intend us to love, to care for, to serve.
Lead us into other people's stories,
that we may build on our shared values
rather than be divided by our differences.
Lord, in your mercy, **hear our prayer.**

We pray for people in need of healing,
comfort, release, and wholeness.
Comfort those who feel trapped
under the rubble of disease, addiction,
pain, poverty, and grief.
Carry away the things that weigh them down,
and lead them into your peace.
Lord, in your mercy, **hear our prayer.**

We offer these prayers in the name of Jesus,
our cornerstone and foundation. **Amen.**

INVITATION TO OFFERING

The invitation to offering may be led from the Communion table.

God tells Moses:
"Speak to all the congregation of the people of Israel
and say to them: You shall be holy,
for I, the Lord your God, am holy.
When you reap the harvest of your land,
you shall not reap to the very edges of your field
or gather the gleanings of your harvest.
You shall not strip your vineyard bare
or gather the fallen grapes of your vineyard;
you shall leave them for the poor and the alien.
I am the Lord your God."

As our offering is received this morning,
we join in God's intention for the world,
where the hungry are fed and the homeless are housed.
Let us offer our gifts as portions of our harvest,
extending our blessings beyond our walls.

INVITATION TO THE TABLE

The invitation to the table is led from the Communion table.

In his first letter to the church in Corinth,
Paul declares that the wisdom of the world
is foolishness to God.
No matter how often the world tells us there isn't enough,
we have this table,
where God's wisdom promises abundance.

Here we gather.
Here we are fed.
Here we are renewed
to offer foolish love and abundance to the world.
Come, be fed, and revel in God's goodness.

CHARGE

The blessing and charge may be led from the doors of the church.

God tells Moses to declare to the people,
"You shall be holy, for I the Lord am holy."
We are invited into holiness
not because we are perfect,
but because we are God's.
Rest in the knowledge that God has claimed you
and calls you holy.
And go out into the world
to spread that holiness, that wholeness,
in a world God already and always loves.
Amen. *or* **Thanks be to God.**

Eighth Sunday after the Epiphany

February 25–29, if before the Transfiguration

Isaiah 49:8–16a
Psalm 131

1 Corinthians 4:1–5
Matthew 6:24–34

OPENING SENTENCES

When we worry that God
couldn't possibly know us or care for us,
God replies through the prophet Isaiah:
"Can a woman forget her nursing child,
or show no compassion for the child of her womb?
Even these may forget, yet I will not forget you.
See, I have inscribed you on the palms of my hands."

Let us worship God.

PRAYER OF THE DAY

Mothering God,
gather us in your arms and hold us.
Calm and quiet our souls like a child with its parent.
Lead us to rest in your embrace
that we may be fed and nurtured here this day
as we worship you with joy and gratitude. **Amen.**

Can a woman forget her nursing child, or show no compassion for the child of her womb? Even these may forget, yet I will not forget you. See, I have inscribed you on the palms of my hands.

Isaiah 49:15–16a

INVITATION TO DISCIPLESHIP

The invitation to discipleship may be led from the baptismal font.

The apostle Paul calls us
"stewards of God's mysteries."
We aren't called to be explainers, debunkers,
or authors of God's mysteries.
We just get to carry the mystery around,
offering it to others,
so God can reveal whatever needs revealing.

We don't promise easy answers or simple platitudes,
but we invite you to join us
as we seek to steward God's mystery as best we can.
There is room for you here with us
to seek, to serve, and to ponder God's mysteries.

PRAYERS OF INTERCESSION

The prayers of intercession may be led from the midst of the congregation.

O God, who turns mountains into roads
and valleys into flat plains,
we come before you in awe and gratitude.
What are humans that you are mindful of us,
mortals that you care for us?
Thank you for holding us close and for caring for us.
We come before you
confessing that we worry too much,
that we borrow worries from the future.
We offer our worries up to you,
author of our lives and bearer of our burdens.
As we set down those things that weigh us down,
may we be freed to pick up the work
you would have us do.

For your church in every place, hear our prayers.
May we shelter and steward your mysteries,
inviting people to join the journey
and giving safety and shelter to those in need.

For your children in every place, hear our prayers.
May we offer your grace and mercy
to a hurting and anxious world.
May we be agents of your justice and hope,
flattening mountains of racism, classism,
and other forms of injustice,
making a clear path for all.

For your created world, hear our prayers.
May we shelter and protect
the beautiful mystery of your creation,
ensuring a safe world for future generations.

For all whose worries are very real,
and caused by illness, grief, and pain, hear our prayers.
Calm and quiet their souls,
as a parent holds and comforts a child.
Bring your healing, your solace, your wholeness,
so the rough places may be made smooth in their lives.

We offer all these prayers
in the name of your Son, Jesus,
who came that we might have life
and have it abundantly. **Amen.**

INVITATION TO OFFERING

The invitation to offering may be led from the Communion table.

Matthew's Gospel teaches us
to look to the birds of the air
when we're worrying about our lives,
what we will eat, what we will wear.
Jesus teaches us to seek God's kingdom first,
and the rest will follow.

As our offering is received this day,
we give with the confidence of God's beloved children.
Out of our abundance may others find hope.

INVITATION TO THE TABLE

The invitation to the table is led from the Communion table.

The prophet Isaiah writes
that God's people "shall feed along the ways,
and on heights shall be their pasture;
they shall not hunger or thirst,
neither scorching wind nor sun shall strike them down.
God, who has pity on them, will lead them,
and by springs of water will guide them."

At this table
we come to understand the promise of Isaiah.
Here we find an abundance, like a pasture.
Here we neither hunger nor thirst.
Here we rest in God's shelter and provision.
So come and be fed.
"For the Lord has comforted the people,
and will have compassion on God's suffering ones."

CHARGE

The blessing and charge may be led from the doors of the church.

Jesus calls us to strive first for the kingdom of God
and God's righteousness,
and all these things will be given to us as well.
This week, may you trust in God's provision
as you seek to bring God's realm
to a worried and anxious world.
Go in peace.
Amen. *or* **Thanks be to God.**

Ninth Sunday after the Epiphany

If the Transfiguration is not observed on the Sunday before Lent begins

Deuteronomy 11:18–21, 26–28   Romans 1:16–17; 3:22b–28 (29–31)
Psalm 31:1–5, 19–24   Matthew 7:21–29

OPENING SENTENCES

In you, O Lord, we seek refuge.
Incline your ear to us.

Rescue us with haste.
You are our rock and our refuge.

Into your hand we commit our spirits,
for you have redeemed us,
O Lord, faithful God.

PRAYER OF THE DAY

O Lord,
our rock and our refuge,
grant us your rest this day.
Draw us into the shelter of your presence,
that we may worship in joy and peace. **Amen.**

"Everyone then who hears these words of mine and acts on them will be like a wise man who built his house on rock. The rain fell, the floods came, and the winds blew and beat on that house, but it did not fall, because it had been founded on rock."

Matthew 7:24–25

INVITATION TO DISCIPLESHIP

The invitation to discipleship may be led from the baptismal font.

In Deuteronomy, God instructs us
to "put these words of mine in your heart and soul,
and you shall bind them as a sign on your hand,
and fix them as an emblem on your forehead."
We're called to teach them to our children,
and to make God's words such a part of our lives
that they are written on our doorposts and our gates.

If you're looking for a community of faith,
where you can learn and study God's words,
where your questions and confusion can be voiced,
please join us as we seek to put God's words
in our hearts and souls.
All of who you are is welcome here.

PRAYERS OF INTERCESSION

The prayers of intercession may be led from the midst of the congregation.

Incline your ear to us, O God,
for you are, indeed,
our rock, our fortress, our salvation.
In the shelter of your presence,
we seek rest from the cares of the world
and the worries of our lives.

We offer to you now our concerns
that are too heavy to carry alone.
Bring peace to troubled hearts,
comfort to those who mourn,
and give healing
to wounded bodies, minds, and spirits.
In you, O Lord, we seek refuge.

In a world beset by storms
of violence, war, and greed,
hear our prayers for people
in the path of disaster, danger, or disease.
May we build a world of shelter
for all of your children
and bring peace to your creation.
In you, O Lord, we seek refuge.

Turn our hearts and spirits toward your Word,
that we may anchor ourselves
to a peace that will last
and a hope that brings life.
Be a rock of refuge for us,
a strong fortress to save us. **Amen.**

INVITATION TO OFFERING

The invitation to offering may be led from the Communion table.

Let us be people who build on solid ground
rather than shifting sand.
Let us give of our time, treasure, and talents
to build a community of justice, peace, and hope.

As our offering is received this day,
let us give generously, with thankful hearts.

INVITATION TO THE TABLE

The invitation to the table is led from the Communion table.

At this table we find refuge and solace.
God is our rock and our fortress,
and at this table we find shelter from the storms.

So come, you who are hungry
and you who know fullness.
Come, you who have great faith
and you who have lots of questions.
Come, you who have been here many times
and you who may be here for the first time.
This is not our table but the Lord's,
and God has set a place for you—yes, you.

CHARGE

The blessing and charge may be led from the doors of the church.

Jesus tells us that if we hear his words and act on them,
we will be like a wise person who built their house on rock.
The rains will still fall, and the floods will still come,
and the winds will still blow and beat on that house,
but it will not fall, because it has been founded on rock.
So go from this place nourished and fed on God's word.
May your actions be a bedrock of peace and hope
in a world beset by storms.
Let us build a world of hope and joy.
Amen. *or* **Thanks be to God.**

Transfiguration Sunday

Sunday before Lent begins

Exodus 24:12–18
Psalm 2 or Psalm 99

2 Peter 1:16–21
Matthew 17:1–9

OPENING SENTENCES

In his farewell to his congregation,
Peter tells his people that as long as he's alive
he'll keep reminding them of the stories of Jesus:
**"For he received honor and glory from God
when that voice was conveyed to him
by the Majestic Glory,
saying, 'This is my Son, my Beloved,
with whom I am well pleased.'"**

Let us tell each other the stories of Jesus again today
as we worship in joy and hope.
It is good for us to be here.

PRAYER OF THE DAY

Holy One,
speak your word into our hearts this day,
that it may kindle a light in us.
May this time of worship
allow us to shelter and tend
the flame of your word,
that it may arise as a morning star in our hearts.
Speak to us again and again,
that we may hear your voice
calling out, "Beloved." **Amen.**

INVITATION TO DISCIPLESHIP

The invitation to discipleship may be led from the baptismal font.

Jesus invited his disciples to join him
on the mountain where he was transfigured.
We too are invited to be witnesses to God's miracles
and overhear the divine conversation.

If you're looking for a community of people
seeking to follow Jesus
up, and then down, the mountain,
we hope you'll join us.

PRAYERS OF INTERCESSION

The prayers of intercession may be led from the midst of the congregation.

Holy God,
your voice cries out from the heavens,
with echoes of "beloved" ringing all around.
Center that voice in us,
that we may know how you love us
deep in our souls,
that we may remember how you love others
deep in our hearts.
God's light goes before us.
Let us walk in the light of the Lord.

Your voice cries out in delight
over your created world,
yet we see profits and ease
instead of delight and wonder.
Forgive our failure to be good stewards
of what you created in love.
God's light goes before us.
Let us walk in the light of the Lord.

Hear our prayers for those places in our world
beset by violence, disaster, heartbreak, and loss.
Speak, again and again,
your voice of love to the lonely,
your voice of hope to the despairing,
and your voice of comfort to the grieving.

Speak your voice of justice to the unjust,
and show us mercy that leads to redemption.
God's light goes before us.
Let us walk in the light of the Lord.

Transfigure your church, O God,
that we may shine with your light
into the shadows of our world.
Transfigure our hearts,
that we may shine with the light of your compassion
as we serve your children.
Transfigure our minds,
that we may see each other
as worthy of love and belonging.
God's light goes before us.
Let us walk in the light of the Lord. Amen.

INVITATION TO OFFERING

The invitation to offering may be led from the Communion table.

Friends, God's word to us
is invitational and never coercive.
We are invited—
both for the journey to the mountaintop
and for the journey to the cross.

As the offering is received this day,
let us respond to God's invitation
and give with hearts that are full
and dreams that are rooted in hope.
Your gifts create the world God is dreaming for us.
Let us join God on this journey.

INVITATION TO THE TABLE

The invitation to the table is led from the Communion table.

We have moments
when we glimpse the dazzling glory of God.
Moses saw God's glory as a cloud of devouring fire.
The disciples saw Jesus transfigured on the mountain.
One of our moments is at this table,
where God sets the table,
where there is always room for more,
where we are fed and sustained for the journey.

Come, be fed, and glimpse the realm of God.

CHARGE

The blessing and charge may be led from the doors of the church.

This week we begin the journey to the cross.
Let us be open to wonder,
that we may glimpse the glory of God.
Let us be committed to justice,
that God's light may shine more brightly in our world.
Let us journey in hope and confidence,
listening for God's voice
crying out "Beloved" as we go.
Amen. *or* **Thanks be to God.**

SEASON OF LENT

Making Connections

In the early history of the church, the season of Lent developed as a time of preparation for baptism at Easter. In the third and fourth centuries, candidates for baptism underwent a period of instruction and examination during the weeks of Lent, and these rites of initiation helped to give shape to what we have come to know as the Lenten season. Lent also has its origins in ancient practices of penance, in which those who had been separated from the community of faith by their sin would seek reconciliation through a time of fasting and prayer. This aspect of the Lenten tradition is especially connected with Jesus' forty days of testing in the wilderness. While these practices continue, the focus of Lent has shifted in many churches toward reflection on the cross, personal spiritual disciplines, and communal preparation for the celebration of Easter.

The Gospel reading for the Second Sunday in Lent helps to connect these historical threads and theological themes. (Matthew 17:1–9 is provided as an alternate reading for churches that commemorate the transfiguration on this day.) Jesus' conversation with Nicodemus (John 3:1–17) begins as a dialogue on baptism: Jesus says, "No one can enter the kingdom of God without being born of water and Spirit" (3:5). Jesus alludes to Israel's wilderness ordeal as prefiguring his crucifixion: "Just as Moses lifted up the serpent in the wilderness, so must the Son of Man be lifted up" (3:14). And then Jesus reveals God's saving purpose: "For God so loved the world . . ." (3:16). As Lent points to Easter, the cross points to everlasting life.

Worship planners may wonder about the Revised Common Lectionary's departure from the Gospel of Matthew for a span of weeks in the season of Lent. On the Third, Fourth, and Fifth Sundays in Lent, we read from the Gospel of John about Jesus' meeting with a woman at a well (John 4:5–42), his healing of a man born blind (John 9:1–41), and his raising of Lazarus from the dead (John 11:1–45). This detour through the Fourth Gospel underscores the Lenten emphasis on baptism by preserving a pattern of readings long connected with the initiation of new believers during the season of Lent.

Draw on these deep baptismal connections as you guide the people of God through the season of Lent. Preach about baptism, using your sacramental imagination in the interpretation of Scripture. Lead worship from the font, as suggested in this book. Include a thanksgiving for baptism during Lent, if you don't already, or a reaffirmation of the baptismal covenant. Use the invitation to discipleship to encourage the not-yet-baptized to seek a deeper relationship with Christ, and the already-baptized to live out the implications of their passage through the waters. Sing from the baptism section of your hymnal. Find occasions to teach about the theology and practice of baptism. Begin a tradition of celebrating baptismal anniversaries in your church.

As you journey through the Lenten wilderness, be sure to bring some (baptismal) water. Stay close to this sacramental source, where the grace of God is "gushing up to eternal life" (John 4:14).

Seasonal/Repeating Resources

These resources are intended for regular use throughout the season of Lent.

The confession and pardon may be led from the baptismal font.

> Remember the words of the psalmist to the people of God:
> Blessed are those whose iniquities are forgiven,
> and whose sins are covered by the grace of God.
>
> Trusting in God's grace, let us confess our sin.

The confession may begin with a time of silence for personal prayer.

> **O Lord our God,**
> **you created us and called us good.**
> **You planted us in the garden of your grace**
> **and provided everything we might need.**
> **Yet we are tempted by other fruit**
> **and succumb to our own desires.**
> **We sin against you,**
> **disobeying your commandments.**
> **We sin against others,**
> **causing sorrow and suffering.**
> **We even sin against ourselves,**
> **forgetting that we are made in your image.**
>
> **Forgive us, O Lord our God.**
> **Deliver us from sin and death,**
> **strengthen us by your faithfulness,**
> **and cover us with your righteousness,**
> **that we may turn away from evil**
> **and live according to your word;**
> **through Jesus Christ our Savior.**

Water may be poured or lifted from the baptismal font.

> Since we are justified by grace through faith,
> we have peace with God in Jesus Christ.
> This is the promise and hope of the gospel—
> and hope does not disappoint us,
> because God's love has been poured into our hearts
> through the gift of the Holy Spirit.

> People of God, believe the good news:
> In the name of Jesus Christ, we are forgiven.
> **Thanks be to God.**

PRAYER FOR ILLUMINATION

The prayer for illumination is led from the lectern or pulpit.

> Speak to us, O Lord.
> Shape us by your Word
> and fill us with your Spirit,
> that these dry bones may rise
> and live to praise your name;
> through Jesus Christ our Savior. **Amen.**

THANKSGIVING FOR BAPTISM

The thanksgiving for baptism is led from the baptismal font.

The introductory dialogue ("The Lord be with you . . .") may be sung or spoken.

> Living God, we give you thanks
> for the living water of our baptism—
> the deep wellspring of your mercy
> gushing up to eternal life.
> You fill the earth with wonder
> and flood the seas with grace.
> You sustain us in the wilderness,
> providing water from a stone.
> You shower us with your Spirit,
> pouring your love into our hearts.
> Continue to fill us with your Spirit,
> and lead us to worship and serve you
> in words and action, spirit and truth,
> until the coming of the Lord Jesus Christ,
> in whose holy name we pray. **Amen.**

GREAT THANKSGIVING

The Great Thanksgiving is led from the Communion table.

The introductory dialogue ("The Lord be with you . . .") may be sung or spoken.

> Glory to you, O God.
> In the beginning, you spoke the Word
> that gave life to all the world.
> You created us in your image
> and called us to be your people.
> Even when we deny your Word
> and betray the promise of our faith,
> you remain faithful in your love.

The Sanctus ("Holy, holy, holy . . .") may be sung or spoken.

> Glory to you, O God.
> You love the world so much
> you sent your only Son to save us.
> Jesus gives living water
> to those who are thirsty.
> He offers healing and grace
> to those who are suffering in sin.
> And to those in the dust of death
> he is the resurrection and the life.

The words of institution are included here, if not elsewhere, while the bread and cup are lifted (but not broken/poured).

> Jesus is the bread of life;
> he is the vine, and we are the branches.
> As we share this bread and cup,
> we offer our lives to you, O God,
> with thanksgiving and praise.

A memorial acclamation ("Christ has died . . .") may be sung or spoken.

Glory to you, O God.
Pour out your Holy Spirit among us.
Transform this simple meal
into the heavenly banquet of grace.
Transform this human gathering
into the living body of Christ.
Teach us to love one another
just as Jesus has loved us,
so all the world will know
that we are Christ's disciples.
Keep us faithful in your service
until, with all the saints, we cry:
"It is finished!" God has done it.

A Trinitarian doxology and Great Amen may be sung or spoken.

PRAYER AFTER COMMUNION

The prayer after Communion is led from the Communion table.

Lord Jesus Christ,
we give you thanks and praise.
At this covenant meal
you have nourished us
with your own body and blood.
Sustain us with your Spirit,
and send us forth singing praise,
until we feast with you again
in the glory of your holy realm. **Amen.**

PRAYER OF THANKSGIVING

The prayer of thanksgiving may be led from the Communion table.

Gracious God, we give you thanks
that through Christ you have taught us
to give without thought of reward,
to be sincere in fasting and prayer,
and to store up treasures in heaven.
Receive the offerings of our lives,
and use these gifts we bring
to help those who are in need,
to do good and relieve suffering,
and to welcome your new creation.
In Jesus' name we pray. **Amen.**

BLESSING

The blessing and charge may be led from the doors of the church.

> May the Lord of heaven and earth
> be your helper as you go forth.
> May the Lord preserve your life
> and protect you from evil.
> May the Lord watch over your going out
> and your coming in, now and always. **Amen.**

The Alleluia in response to the blessing is traditionally omitted in Lent.

Ash Wednesday

Joel 2:1–2, 12–17 *or*
 Isaiah 58:1–12
Psalm 51:1–17

2 Corinthians 5:20b–6:10
Matthew 6:1–6, 16–21

The liturgy for Ash Wednesday marks the beginning of Lent, a season of penitence and preparation for Easter. On Ash Wednesday we confront the hard realities of human finitude and failure, confessing our dependence on divine grace for salvation from sin and death.

The primary theological themes of Ash Wednesday include repentance from sin, renewal of spiritual disciplines, and reconciliation with God and neighbor. Distinctive elements of the liturgy are the invitation to observe a holy Lent, the litany of penitence (in combination with Psalm 51), and the imposition of ashes.

The resources that follow are intended to offer creativity, flexibility, and additional options for the church's celebration of Ash Wednesday. Selected texts may be incorporated into the liturgies provided in denominational service books, such as the Presbyterian Church (U.S.A.) *Book of Common Worship* (pp. 247–57). Or they may be used in combination with other materials, found in this book or elsewhere, to develop new liturgies for Ash Wednesday.

OPENING SENTENCES

God says, "I have listened to you;
on the day of salvation I have helped you."
Now is the acceptable time;
now is the day of salvation!

Let us seek God,
delighting to know God's ways.

PRAYER OF THE DAY

Eternal Spirit,
in whom we find our treasure,
create clean hearts in us today
that we might be reconciled to you
and forevermore declare your praise. **Amen.**

INVITATION TO DISCIPLESHIP
AND INVITATION TO OBSERVE A HOLY LENT

The invitation to discipleship may be led from the baptismal font.

We are invited to a fast
by a God who loves justice
and desires freedom and plenty for all people.

We are invited to join in the work
of sharing our food with the hungry,
satisfying the needs of the afflicted,
and turning away from serving only our own interests.

As we enter the season of Lent,
let us seek God not just in our thoughts
but in our actions.

PRAYERS OF INTERCESSION

The prayers of intercession may be led from the midst of the congregation.

God, our guide and guardian,
we are people of your promises,
but we have known hardship.
Knowing that you have accompanied your people
through difficulties beyond our imagining,
we bring our own trials to you.

We pray for those who are imprisoned,
for those whose work drains them more than it fulfills them,
for those who spend sleepless nights
wondering how to move forward,
for those who wonder when or if their next meal will come,
for those who feel like they will never be enough,
for those who ache with physical or mental pain,
for those who are nearing the end of their time on this earth.

You are the one who is here with us
in all of our hardships.

We pray that you might bless us
with knowledge, patience, kindness,
holiness of spirit,
genuine love,
truthful speech,
and your divine power
that turns sorrow to rejoicing. **Amen.**

INVITATION TO OFFERING

The invitation to offering may be led from the Communion table.

We give not to show off our piety,
not to claim righteousness,
but to show our gratitude to God
as we store up treasures in heaven.

With willing spirits
let us offer our gifts to God.

INVITATION TO THE TABLE

The invitation to the table is led from the Communion table.

Even when we have lost our way,
God calls us back,
guiding us,
restoring us,
cleansing us,
rebuilding us.

Here at this table
God's promises still await us.
Come.
Return.
Feast.

CHARGE

The blessing and charge may be led from the doors of the church.

Go forth in peace
and be guided by God.
Amen. *or* **Thanks be to God.**

First Sunday in Lent

Genesis 2:15–17; 3:1–7   Romans 5:12–19
Psalm 32   Matthew 4:1–11

OPENING SENTENCES

Happy are those who trust in the Lord.
God's steadfast love surrounds us.

May we be glad and rejoice.
Let us worship the Lord together!

PRAYER OF THE DAY

Faithful God,
we seek to follow the ways of your Son, Jesus.
Cleanse our hearts and minds
from all that might be a distraction.
Renew in us a desire to worship you,
so we may be an example
of your love and grace to the world.
In the name of Christ we pray. **Amen.**

INVITATION TO DISCIPLESHIP

The invitation to discipleship may be led from the baptismal font.

Jesus said: "One does not live by bread alone,
but by every word that comes from the mouth of God."

If you are tired and weary
from the temptations of the world,
we welcome you to come and find rest
in this community of faith.

PRAYERS OF INTERCESSION

The prayers of intercession may be led from the midst of the congregation.

With the assurance that God will hear us,
we lift up our prayers for the world.
Let us pray.

We lift up prayers for the world . . .
Lord, in your mercy, **hear our prayer.**

We lift up prayers for our nation . . .
Lord, in your mercy, **hear our prayer.**

We lift up prayers for those who are sick . . .
Lord, in your mercy, **hear our prayer.**

We lift up prayers for those living in poverty . . .
Lord, in your mercy, **hear our prayer.**

We lift up prayers for those who are facing temptation . . .
Lord, in your mercy, **hear our prayer.**

We lift up prayers for the church of Jesus Christ in all lands . . .
Lord, in your mercy, **hear our prayer.**

Receive our prayers, O Lord.
Assure us as we go forth into the world
that you have heard and will answer us in due time.
In the name of Christ we pray. **Amen.**

INVITATION TO OFFERING

The invitation to offering may be led from the Communion table.

All that we have and all that we own
are gifts from God.
Let us prepare to return a portion
of what God has given us
as an expression of our gratitude.

INVITATION TO THE TABLE

The invitation to the table is led from the Communion table.

Beloved, let us rejoice!
We do so because we are invited to this table
to partake of the gifts
God has given us in Jesus Christ.
We are here not because of our own doing,
but through the gift of grace.

Let us rejoice and be glad
as we gather at the table.

CHARGE

The blessing and charge may be led from the doors of the church.

May we go forth to worship and serve
the Lord our God—and only God.
Amen. *or* **Thanks be to God.**

Second Sunday in Lent

Genesis 12:1–4a   Romans 4:1–5, 13–17
Psalm 121   John 3:1–17 *or* Matthew 17:1–9

OPENING SENTENCES

I lift up my eyes to the hills—
from where will my help come?

My help comes from the Lord,
who made heaven and earth.

PRAYER OF THE DAY

O Lord,
as we gather here to worship in this place,
assure us of your presence through the Holy Spirit,
that we may be led to follow you
this day and always.
In the name of Christ we pray. **Amen.**

INVITATION TO DISCIPLESHIP

The invitation to discipleship may be led from the baptismal font.

Beloved, we come to Christ by faith.
The good news and fellowship of God
is now extended to you.

If you wish to become a part of this faith community,
we welcome you now, as Christ welcomes you.

PRAYERS OF INTERCESSION

The prayers of intercession may be led from the midst of the congregation.

We are in the presence of a loving God
who invites us to pray for ourselves and others.
Let us pray.

O Lord, we pray for those who have lost loved ones . . .
Assure them that death never has the final word,
for the resurrection of Christ gives us hope.

O Lord, we pray for nations in conflict . . .
May all discord and strife cease,
so that your peace will dwell within us.

O Lord, we pray for our community . . .
May your Holy Spirit be with everyone
as we seek to live together in peace and harmony.

O Lord, we pray for the earth and its resources . . .
May we be stewards of your creation
and preserve the earth's resources,
so that all may have enough.

O Lord, we pray for loved ones . . .
Grant your direction to all who are lost and lonely.
Assure them they do not walk alone,
for you are always with them.

Create in us clean hearts and renew our spirits,
that as we go forth into the world
we may proclaim your glory.
In the name of Christ we pray. **Amen.**

INVITATION TO OFFERING

The invitation to offering may be led from the Communion table.

God's mercies are new every day.
As we remember
what God has done, is doing, and will do,
let us return our gifts and talents back to God
through the offering of our lives.

INVITATION TO THE TABLE

The invitation to the table is led from the Communion table.

Hear the good news:
"For God so loved the world
that he gave his only Son,
so that everyone who believes in him
may not perish but may have eternal life."

Praise the Lord!
The Lord loves us so much
that through the grace of God
we are invited to this table.
Let us share in the feast God has prepared.

CHARGE

The blessing and charge may be led from the doors of the church.

A voice from heaven speaks:
"This is my Son, the Beloved;
with him I am well pleased; listen to him!"
Let us go forth to listen
for the voice of our Savior, Jesus Christ.
Amen. *or* **Thanks be to God.**

Third Sunday in Lent

Exodus 17:1–7

Romans 5:1–11

Psalm 95

John 4:5–42

OPENING SENTENCES

Come, let us sing to the Lord!
Let us make a joyful noise
to the rock of our salvation!

Come, let us worship and bow down.
Let us kneel before the Lord, our Maker!

PRAYER OF THE DAY

Loving God,
as we gather for worship today,
we are tired, weary, and seeking solace.
Refresh us with your Holy Spirit,
the living water,
so we may hear your word
and pledge ourselves to serve you.
In the name of Christ we pray. **Amen.**

INVITATION TO DISCIPLESHIP

The invitation to discipleship may be led from the baptismal font.

Remember the promise of Scripture:
"God proves God's love for us
in that while we still were sinners
Christ died for us."
God's love continually calls us
into deeper relationship.

If you are ready to respond to God's call,
we invite you to become a follower of Jesus
in this community of faith.

PRAYERS OF INTERCESSION

The prayers of intercession may be led from the midst of the congregation.

O God, you have taught us
not only to pray for ourselves
but for others and for the world.
Hear us now as we lift up our prayers.

We pray for peace . . .
Inspire us to be peacemakers,
as Christ taught us.

We pray for those in authority . . .
Guide them through your Holy Spirit
that they may discern your will for all people
in their decisions.

We pray for those who are oppressed . . .
Break the chains of bondage
and set them free.

We pray for the lost . . .
Direct them by the Holy Spirit
to a place of rest and security.

We pray for the church . . .
Empower us who claim to follow you
that we will be your presence
wherever we go.

Assure us, O God,
that our prayers are not in vain.
Strengthen us to abide in faith,
and give us endurance
until we witness the coming of your kingdom.
In Christ's name we pray. **Amen.**

INVITATION TO OFFERING

The invitation to offering may be led from the Communion table.

> The law of God teaches us:
> "All shall give as they are able,
> according to the blessing
> that the Lord your God has given you."
>
> Let us return our gifts and talents to the Lord
> through the receiving of our offering.

INVITATION TO THE TABLE

The invitation to the table is led from the Communion table.

> O taste and see that the Lord is good!
> Happy are those who find refuge in God!
>
> The Lord is good and merciful to us.
> You are invited to this table
> in response to God's graciousness.
> Come, partake of the gifts of God.

CHARGE

The blessing and charge may be led from the doors of the church.

> Receive the living water
> Christ has provided.
> Go forth and tell others the good news.
> **Amen.** *or* **Thanks be to God.**

Fourth Sunday in Lent

1 Samuel 16:1–13   Ephesians 5:8–14
Psalm 23   John 9:1–41

OPENING SENTENCES

The Lord shepherds us.
God restores our souls.

We shall not fear evil.
For God is always with us.

PRAYER OF THE DAY

Faithful God, we profess
that you are the light of the world.
Empower us through our worship of you today,
that we may live as children of the light
and be faithful witnesses to your love in the world.
We pray this through Jesus Christ our Lord. **Amen.**

INVITATION TO DISCIPLESHIP

The invitation to discipleship may be led from the baptismal font.

The Lord does not look on our outward appearance
but looks on our hearts.

The time has come and is near
for those who wish to belong
to this community of believers.
If you are willing, we welcome you.

PRAYERS OF INTERCESSION

The prayers of intercession may be led from the midst of the congregation.

Remembering the grace of God,
who calls us to lay down our burdens,
let us lift up prayers for ourselves and others.
Let us pray.

O God, we pray for our world,
that we may be responsible stewards of your creation . . .

O God, we pray for our loved ones,
that your presence will surround them . . .

O God, we pray for those who hunger and thirst,
that you may provide for their daily sustenance . . .

O God, we pray for churches,
that we may be empowered to do your will . . .

O God, we pray for all humanity,
that all may live in peace and harmony . . .

O God, we pray for those who are dying,
that you will assure them of your presence . . .

We thank you, O God, for hearing our prayers.
May we live in faith,
rejoicing in the power of your Holy Spirit.
In the name of Christ we pray. **Amen.**

INVITATION TO OFFERING

The invitation to offering may be led from the Communion table.

The Scriptures tell us that
in the time of the ancient temple,
the faithful brought their contributions and tithes
and dedicated them to God.

Let us offer our gifts and lives to the Lord.

INVITATION TO THE TABLE

The invitation to the table is led from the Communion table.

Jesus says, "Come to me,
all you that are weary
and are carrying heavy burdens,
and I will give you rest."

**Jesus says, "Take my yoke upon you,
and learn from me;
for I am gentle and humble in heart,
and you will find rest for your souls."**

CHARGE

The blessing and charge may be led from the doors of the church.

May you walk in the presence of the Lord
all the days of your life.
Amen. *or* **Thanks be to God.**

Fifth Sunday in Lent

Ezekiel 37:1–14   Romans 8:6–11
Psalm 130   John 11:1–45

OPENING SENTENCES

O people of God, hope in the Lord!
For with God there is steadfast love
and great power to redeem.

Wait for the Lord.
Our souls wait for the Lord
more than those who watch for the morning.

PRAYER OF THE DAY

O God who weeps with us,
you have sat beside us in the depths,
waiting with us in every dry and lifeless valley.
Grant us the endurance to wait as you do,
to discern in breathless bones the beginning of new life
and in days-old tombs a coming resurrection,
while never bypassing the reality of grief
or rushing those who yearn for comfort.
Breathe in us your life-giving Spirit,
that we might live and wait.
Through Jesus Christ we pray. **Amen.**

INVITATION TO DISCIPLESHIP

The invitation to discipleship may be led from the baptismal font.

Just as God commanded Ezekiel to prophesy to dry bones,
so we are called to sit with the death that we encounter.

In what ways are you being invited
not only into awareness of new life
but also into an acquaintance with grief?

PRAYERS OF INTERCESSION

The prayers of intercession may be led from the midst of the congregation.

Spirit of the living God,
we cry to you out of the depths.
Hear our voice!
Be attentive to our cry!
We live in the gap between resurrections,
longing to hear you speak life to our weary souls:
our souls wait for you,
more than those who watch for the morning.

We cry out with those whose bones are dried up,
suffering from chronic illnesses,
the persistent weight of oppression,
and the ongoing effects of poverty.
As we cry out with them,
our souls wait for you,
more than those who watch for the morning.

We raise our voices with those whose hope is lost,
weighed down by the ebb and flow of grief,
in despair at the state of this world you have made,
and exhausted by violence and abuse.
As we raise our voices with them,
our souls wait for you,
more than those who watch for the morning.

We sit in solidarity with those who feel cut off completely,
mired in the depths of loneliness,
relegated to the margins of society,
shunned and forgotten by those who should love them.
As we sit with them,
our souls wait for you,
more than those who watch for the morning.

O great advocate and comforter,
through your radiant presence
teach us that the sorrows that grieve us
disturb your Spirit too.
Enliven our spirits with your steadfast love,
even as we wait for your redemption.
Through Jesus Christ we pray. **Amen.**

INVITATION TO OFFERING

The invitation to offering may be led from the Communion table.

As God called Ezekiel to practice his ministry of prophecy
among skulls and skeletons,
so we are called to offer what we have,
participating in the Spirit's redemptive, restorative work.

INVITATION TO THE TABLE

The invitation to the table is led from the Communion table.

Jesus, the resurrection and the life,
who sheds tears of grief and wipes ours from our eyes,
invites us to this table of grace,
where there is a feast of rich food
and the promise of death is swallowed up forever.

CHARGE

The blessing and charge may be led from the doors of the church.

As your souls wait
for God's coming redemption,
may you sit with the bones,
weep with those who are grieving,
and cry out with those in the depths.
Amen. *or* **Thanks be to God.**

Liturgy of the Palms/Passion

LITURGY OF THE PALMS
Psalm 118:1–2, 19–29
Matthew 21:1–11

LITURGY OF THE PASSION
Isaiah 50:4–9a
Psalm 31:9–16
Philippians 2:5–11
Matthew 26:14–27:66 *or*
Matthew 27:11–54

The liturgy for Palm/Passion Sunday is designed for a day of stark contrast, a drama in two acts. It begins with a joyful procession into Jerusalem but ends with the somber journey to the cross. Worship planners are advised to resist the urge to avoid the theological tension inherent in the day by choosing between the palms and the passion. Rather, the fullness of Christian faith requires that we face the discomfort and live into the tension for the integrity of the gospel and for the sake of the world God loves.

The primary theological themes of Palm/Passion Sunday include the identity of the Suffering Servant and the ironic triumph and tragedy of Jesus' death, as shouts of celebration and a welcome fit for a king turn into cries of derision and a crown of thorns. Distinctive elements of the liturgy are the procession with palms and the poignant and extensive proclamation of Jesus' suffering and death; due to the nature and length of the Gospel reading, on Palm/Passion Sunday a brief sermon or time of contemplative silence may complete the proclamation of the word.

The resources that follow are intended to offer creativity, flexibility, and additional options for the church's celebration of Palm/Passion Sunday. Selected texts may be incorporated into the liturgies provided in denominational service books, such as the Presbyterian Church (U.S.A.) *Book of Common Worship* (pp. 263–71). Or they may be used in combination with other materials, found in this book or elsewhere, to develop new liturgies for Palm/Passion Sunday.

OPENING SENTENCES

O give thanks to the Lord, for God is good.
God's steadfast love endures forever.

The stone that the builders rejected
has become the chief cornerstone!
Hosanna in the highest!

Fling wide the gates,
that all may enter in and give God thanks.
God's steadfast love endures forever.

Blessed are all who come in the name of the Lord!
Hosanna in the highest!

PRAYER OF THE DAY

God of the humbled and rejected,
you did not exploit your divine position or power
but, faithful in your love,
came as a human to live among us,
spending your life with outcasts and sinners
and opening gates that long had been closed.
You were mocked and insulted,
denied and betrayed,
spat upon and beaten,
convicted and crucified
for claiming a kin-dom
of the lost and forsaken.
Make us bold to follow you,
to set our faces like flint
toward your coming kin-dom
of justice, righteousness, and peace,
where those who have been rejected
are considered indispensable.
All this we pray through Jesus Christ,
our cornerstone. **Amen.**

INVITATION TO DISCIPLESHIP

The invitation to discipleship may be led from the baptismal font.

Through his life, teachings, death, and resurrection,
Jesus taught us how to sustain the weary with a word
and stand together with those who face disgrace.

Will we become disciples of God's continuing ministry
of relieving suffering and siding with the rejected,
even if it means experiencing suffering ourselves?

PRAYERS OF INTERCESSION

The prayers of intercession may be led from the midst of the congregation.

O God, be gracious to us.
Like those who raised palms
and spread their coats before you,
we lift up to you this weary world
and lay down our burdens before you.
We acknowledge that you are the one who comes to help.
We trust in you, O Lord;
we have said, "You are our God."
Hear our prayers.

We lift up to you those wasting away in grief,
whose years are spent in sorrow . . .
O God, **be gracious to us.**

We lift up to you those whose bones ache,
whose bodies have become like broken vessels . . .
O God, **be gracious to us.**

We lift up to you those who have been forsaken,
who pass out of our collective minds,
whose neighbors turn their face from them in horror . . .
O God, **be gracious to us.**

We lift up to you those who face terror all around,
who experience violence of all kinds . . .
O God, **be gracious to us.**

We lift up to you this world, groaning under the weight
of our exploitation and greed . . .
O God, **be gracious to us.**

Loving God,
you are not a stranger to distress.
Our times are in your hand;
you embrace our daily sorrows.
In your steadfast love
let your face shine upon us,
and grant us your peace.
Keep us awake to the suffering of those around us,
even as we experience your healing;
through Jesus Christ our Lord. **Amen.**

INVITATION TO OFFERING

The invitation to offering may be led from the Communion table.

In gratitude to the God
who has given us light
and done marvelous things,
let us give of ourselves
and join in what God is doing.

INVITATION TO THE TABLE

The invitation to the table is led from the Communion table.

This is God's table,
where the righteous and the rejected
are invited to eat and be satisfied.
Come, disciples of the crucified one,
all has been made ready.

CHARGE

The blessing and charge may be led from the doors of the church.

Stay awake to the suffering
of those who have been rejected and forsaken.
Make space in your lives
and at your tables
for the broken one who comes to make us whole.
Amen. *or* **Thanks be to God.**

The Three Days

The liturgy for the Three Days (or *Triduum*)—Holy Thursday, Good Friday, and the Great Vigil of Easter—is best understood as a single service in three parts. Together these events proclaim the mystery that is at the center of the church's calendar and the heart of Christian faith—the death and resurrection of Jesus Christ.

The primary theological themes of Holy Thursday include Christ's example of humble service and self-giving love. Distinctive elements of the liturgy are the act of foot washing and the celebration of the Eucharist or Lord's Supper, as well as the stripping of the church (removal of symbols and paraments) that may happen at its conclusion. The primary theological themes of Good Friday include God's compassion for the world, expressed through Jesus' passion on the cross, and the paradoxical nature of the atonement: strength from weakness, salvation from suffering, good from evil. Distinctive elements of the liturgy are the expansive prayers of intercession and Christ's lament in the solemn reproaches of the cross. The primary theological themes of the Great Vigil of Easter include God's saving work through history, culminating in Christ's resurrection, and the formation of church as covenant community and body of Christ. Distinctive elements of the liturgy are its four movements (Light, Readings, Baptism, and Eucharist) and its organization as a pilgrimage of the people of God.

The resources that follow are intended to offer creativity, flexibility, and additional options for the church's celebration of Holy Thursday, Good Friday, and the Great Vigil of Easter. Selected texts may be incorporated into the liturgies provided in denominational service books, such as the Presbyterian Church (U.S.A.) *Book of Common Worship* (pp. 272–304). Or they may be used in combination with other materials, found in this book or elsewhere, to develop new liturgies for the Three Days.

Holy Thursday

Exodus 12:1–4 (5–10), 11–14   1 Corinthians 11:23–26
Psalm 116:1–2, 12–19   John 13:1–17, 31b–35

OPENING SENTENCES

> Praise the Lord!
> In the courts of the house of God,
> **praise the Lord!**
>
> In the presence of God's people,
> **praise the Lord!**
>
> For all that God has done for us,
> **praise the Lord!**

PRAYER OF THE DAY

> Humble Savior,
> who stoops to wash our feet,
> open us to the closeness you long to share with us,
> the wisdom you seek to give to us,
> and the love you willingly pour out for us,
> that you may be glorified through us
> in our day and age. **Amen.**

"I give you a new commandment, that you love one another. Just as I have loved you, you also should love one another. By this everyone will know that you are my disciples, if you have love for one another."

John 13:34–35

INVITATION TO DISCIPLESHIP

The invitation to discipleship may be led from a foot-washing basin or from the baptismal font.

Jesus does not yell or force his followers
to do what he asks.
Jesus gently offers a new way,
marked by care and love,
and invites them, once again, to follow.

This invitation echoes in us today.
If it resonates in your soul, consider:
What does it look like
for you to live out this love?
What does it look like
for you to follow in the example
of a leader who washes his disciples' feet?

PRAYERS OF INTERCESSION

The prayers of intercession may be led from the midst of the congregation.

Servant God,
we take this time to pause
on the journey toward the cross.
We take this time to remember
that you have bound us together in love.
You define us by love.

As we hold this ritual remembrance,
we seek signs of your presence in our time.

Give a sign to all whose stomachs rumble
and throats thirst.
Give a sign to all for whom more is uncertain
than trusted and known.
Give a sign to all who are isolated
and long for your presence.
Give a sign to all who mourn,
whose tears are not easily wiped away.
Give a sign to all who feel unworthy
of the Savior who washes our feet,
who makes a way to freedom for us.

By these signs, inspire us
to take up not just the cross but the towel,
that we might move forward with humility,
sharing the love that we have received. **Amen.**

INVITATION TO OFFERING

The invitation to offering may be led from the Communion table.

What shall we return to God
for all the goodness we have received?

We offer our vows, our gifts, our sacrifices to God.

INVITATION TO THE TABLE

The invitation to the table is led from the Communion table.

This story,
of how Jesus Christ took bread and cup,
and blessed them
and shared them,
sharing his very self with us,
has been passed down from generation to generation.

This invitation,
to eat and drink
and proclaim,
is extended through the ages
from Jesus Christ himself,
who offers us grace and forgiveness,
no matter what betrayals we bring to the table.

Come.
This table is for all of us.

CHARGE

The blessing and charge may be led from the doors of the church.

Go forth in love,
loving one another,
so everyone might know
you a disciple of Jesus Christ.
Amen. *or* **Thanks be to God.**

The service continues on Good Friday.

Good Friday

Isaiah 52:13–53:12
Psalm 22

Hebrews 10:16–25 *or*
    Hebrews 4:14–16; 5:7–9
John 18:1–19:42

OPENING SENTENCES

We come to stand in awe of God,
who hears us when we cry.

All the ends of the earth will remember
and turn to the Lord.
**As Christ died for us,
we shall live for Christ.**

PRAYER OF THE DAY

Startling Savior,
we come to remember this agonizing night:
the night when you were wounded,
crushed, delivered to death.
Although we did not stay with you,
stay with us,
that we might never forsake you,
but follow in your footsteps
to the foot of the cross. **Amen.**

I can count all my bones. They stare and gloat over me; they divide my clothes among themselves, and for my clothing they cast lots. But you, O LORD, do not be far away! O my help, come quickly to my aid!

Psalm 22:17–19

INVITATION TO DISCIPLESHIP

The invitation to discipleship may be led from the baptismal font.

This story seems impossible to believe:
a story of love that faces death,
a story of sinful hearts sprinkled clean,
a story of a new and living way opened for us.

Let us not simply be hearers of the word but doers:
How can we provoke ourselves and one another
to love and good deeds?
How can we encourage each other
on the path Christ has opened for us?

PRAYERS OF INTERCESSION

The prayers of intercession may be led from the midst of the congregation.

O God,
to whom our ancestors cried,
it seems selfish to ask anything of you now.
Here, on this day when we remember
the great sacrifice you made for us,
how could we ask for anything else?
And yet . . .

Salvation has come, and yet
the earth groans under the weight of abuse.
Salvation has come, and yet
people buckle under the weight of oppression.
Salvation has come, and yet
friends and family cry out under the weight of illness.
Salvation has come, and yet
the world is not yet whole.

So the work continues.
The work you began and invited us into
must keep moving on.

On this day we are bold to ask
for you to guide us
along this difficult road you know so well,
for you to comfort us
when the terrors of this world become too much,
for you to strengthen us
to be able to face what lies ahead,
for you to call us back
when we are too scared to keep going,
for you to be with us, now and always,
as we try, and fail, and try again
to be your people in this world. **Amen.**

SOLEMN REPROACHES OF THE CROSS

O my people,
what more could I have done for you?
Answer me!

I created you in my image,
but you do not recognize me
when you encounter people
whose skin color, sexuality, or politics
are different from yours.
I breathed my Spirit of welcome into your lungs,
and you breathe out hatred and division.
You have made a cross for your Savior.
Holy God,
we are poured out like water.
Holy immortal One,
have mercy upon us.

I delivered you out of slavery,
and you have created, and profited from,
a world where people are still enslaved.
Nobody is free until everyone is free.
You have made a cross for your Savior.
Holy God,
we are poured out like water.
Holy immortal One,
have mercy upon us.

I planted you as my vineyard,
nurturing your growth and watering your roots,
but you have yielded rotten fruit.
You have not nurtured the earth entrusted to your care.
You have exploited creation as if it were yours.
I created you as branches,
and you thought you were the vine.
You have made a cross for your Savior.
Holy God,
we are poured out like water.
Holy immortal One,
have mercy upon us.

I walked before you as cloud and fire,
guiding your journey.
I made a way where there was no way,
leading you through water on dry land,
but you refuse to help others on their journeys,
building walls instead of bridges.
You have made a cross for your Savior.
Holy God,
we are poured out like water.
Holy immortal One,
have mercy upon us.

I asked you to rend your hearts and not your garments,
but you have made public displays of thoughts and prayers
and have not let your hearts be moved
by the violence that plagues your streets,
your theaters, your schools, your churches.
I told Peter to put down his sword,
but you have armed yourselves
and sought peace through violence.
You have made a cross for your Savior.
Holy God,
we are poured out like water.
Holy immortal One,
have mercy upon us.

I moved into the neighborhood, full of grace and truth,
but people remain on the streets
because housing is not available, not affordable,
in a world of growing inequality.
Where could the Word made flesh afford to lay his head today?
You have made a cross for your Savior.
Holy God,
we are poured out like water.
Holy immortal One,
have mercy upon us.

I was a stranger and you did not welcome me,
naked and you did not give me clothing,
sick and in prison and you did not visit me,
hungry and you did not feed me,
thirsty and you did not give me a drink.
You have made a cross for your Savior.
Holy God,
we are poured out like water.
Holy immortal One,
have mercy upon us.

The service continues at the Great Vigil of Easter or on the Resurrection of the Lord.

Great Vigil of Easter

Twelve readings from the Hebrew Scriptures are provided for the Service of Readings in the Great Vigil of Easter. At least three should be chosen; the Exodus reading is always included. Psalms or canticles are provided as a musical response to each reading.

1. Genesis 1:1–2:4a
   Psalm 136:1–9, 23–26
2. Genesis 7:1–5, 11–18; 8:6–18; 9:8–13
   Psalm 46
3. Genesis 22:1–18
   Psalm 16
4. Exodus 14:10–31; 15:20–21
   Exodus 15:1b–13, 17–18
5. Baruch 3:9–15; 3:32–4:4 *or* Proverbs 8:1–8, 19–21; 9:4b–6
   Psalm 19
6. Isaiah 55:1–11
   Isaiah 12:2–6
7. Isaiah 61:1–4, 9–11
   Deuteronomy 32:1–4, 7, 36a, 43a
8. Ezekiel 36:24–28
   Psalms 42 and 43
9. Ezekiel 37:1–14
   Psalm 143
10. Daniel 3:1–29
    Song of the Three 35–65
11. Jonah 1:1–2:1
    Jonah 2:2–3 (4–6), 7–9
12. Zephaniah 3:14–20
    Psalm 98

The Service of Readings continues with the Epistle (and its Psalm response) and Gospel:

Romans 6:3–11
Psalm 114
John 20:1–18

OPENING SENTENCES

Do not be afraid. Stand firm.
**See the deliverance
that the Lord will accomplish today.**

The Lord our God is in our midst,
renewing us with love.
**God rejoices over us with gladness,
and we will sing to our Lord!**

PRAYER OF THE DAY

God of creation and covenant,
who has always saved us
and provided for us
and delivered us:
Surprise us once again by your resurrection,
that we might be free from death
and alive in you. **Amen.**

INVITATION TO DISCIPLESHIP

The invitation to discipleship may be led from the baptismal font.

In this new day,
we have died and now we live.
We are alive to the possibility of peace.
We are alive to a dream of freedom.
We are alive to God in Jesus Christ.

If you desire this life,
let us join together
to walk side by side
in newness of life with Christ Jesus.

*A prayer of thanksgiving over the water or thanksgiving for baptism
follows.*

PRAYERS OF INTERCESSION

The prayers of intercession may be led from the midst of the congregation.

God, whose steadfast love endures forever,
we come with joy to behold your works,
to witness your resurrection,
and to praise your holy name.
Living Savior, **raise us to new life in you.**

When we are trapped in our own tombs
of illness, hunger, addiction, or despair:
Living Savior, **raise us to new life in you.**

When we are the ones yelling, "Crucify!"
hurting others, harming your creation:
Living Savior, **raise us to new life in you.**

When we cannot believe the good news,
feeling hopeless and helpless:
Living Savior, **raise us to new life in you.**

When we are mourning those we've lost,
with pain poisoning our good memories:
Living Savior, **raise us to new life in you.**

When we are frightened by sudden change,
unable to see the possibilities ahead:
Living Savior, **raise us to new life in you.**

Bring us home, resurrected Christ.
Gather us, restore us,
raise us to new life in you. **Amen.**

INVITATION TO OFFERING

The invitation to offering may be led from the Communion table.

God is our strength and our might
and has become our salvation.
With joy we give thanks to our God,
shouting aloud and singing our praises.

With these gifts
we proclaim that God has done great things for us
and is worthy of our worship, praise, and offering.

INVITATION TO THE TABLE

The invitation to the table is led from the Communion table.

The God who created the heavens and the earth,
the Holy One who parted the waters of the Red Sea,
the Savior who died for us and rose again,
is the one who sets this table.

God sets a feast before us,
inviting everyone who is hungry and thirsty
to come, to eat, to delight.

CHARGE

The blessing and charge may be led from the doors of the church.

Do not be afraid;
go and tell the good news:
Jesus is risen!
Amen. *or* **Thanks be to God.**

SEASON OF EASTER

Making Connections

The season of Easter is a time for celebration—a fifty-day "festival" between the Resurrection of the Lord and the Day of Pentecost. The early church leader Tertullian (c. 155–220) referred to it as the "most joyful space" in the church's year, a time especially appropriate for celebrating the sacrament of baptism. The First Council of Nicaea (325), best known for the Nicene Creed, even sought to enact a spirit of jubilation by forbidding the practice of kneeling (associated with penitential prayer) during the seven weeks of Easter.

The second reading for the Second Sunday of Easter in Revised Common Lectionary Year A perfectly expresses the exultation of the Easter season: "Blessed be the God and Father of our Lord Jesus Christ! By his great mercy he has given us a new birth into a living hope through the resurrection of Jesus Christ from the dead, and into an inheritance that is imperishable, undefiled, and unfading" (1 Pet. 1:3–4). The season of Easter sets aside a span of time for celebrating our "new birth" as believers. It provides a joyful space for living into—and living out of—our "living hope" as the people of God. This season stretches out for a "week of weeks" because it is an emblem of eternal life: "imperishable, undefiled, and unfading."

The Easter season in Year A features a series of six readings from this ancient letter, the first of two epistles attributed to the apostle Peter. Written in a situation of suffering and scorn, 1 Peter reflects the struggles of early Christians to proclaim the good news of Jesus' resurrection in the face of opposition and derision. Understanding the context only amplifies the "living hope" this epistle seeks to instill. The letter calls Christians to a new and holy way of life (1 Pet. 1:17–23) as a "royal priesthood" and "God's own people" (2:1–10). It offers encouragement to those who are persecuted (2:19–25) because they are living according to their faith (3:13–22), urging them to remain steadfast as they await the coming of Christ in glory (4:12–14; 5:6–11). The epistle reading for the Fourth Sunday of Easter comes out of sequence so as to align the image of Christ as "shepherd and guardian of your souls" (2:25) with Psalm 23 and John 10:1–10 (the shepherd and the gate).

As you shepherd the people of God through the fifty days of Easter, make space for resurrection joy. Imagine what it might be like for the celebration of "Easter Sunday" (a misnomer, since there are eight of them, including the Day of Pentecost) to continue and even grow throughout the Easter season. Plan sermons, liturgy, music, and visual art that will connect from week to week, conveying a sense of ongoing and expansive celebration. Find ways to enact this exultation with gestures, postures, or actions that embody joy. At the same time, never let shouts of laughter drown out cries of pain. As 1 Peter demonstrates, the good news of new life and hope in Christ is especially intended for those who are suffering. Be sure your congregation's celebration of Easter also makes space for ministries of justice and reconciliation. If the Easter season is a time for the renewal of worship, it should also be a time of recommitment to service with people who are oppressed and in need.

Christ is risen! God "has given us a new birth into a living hope through the resurrection of Jesus Christ from the dead" (1 Pet. 1:3). Christ is risen indeed! Alleluia! Amen.

Seasonal/Repeating Resources

These resources are intended for regular use throughout the season of Easter.

CONFESSION AND PARDON

The confession and pardon may be led from the baptismal font.

God is our rock and our fortress,
who protects us from danger
and saves us from death.

In confidence and faith in God's mercy,
let us confess our misdeeds
that we may receive grace.

The confession may begin with a time of silence for personal prayer.

**Gracious God,
you give us new life, but we choose the ways of death.
You breathe peace upon us, yet we pursue conflict.
You seek us out when we are afraid, yet we cling to our fears.**

**Forgive us for turning away from you.
Shine your light upon us
and banish all shadows,
that we may live faithfully and joyfully for you.**

Water may be poured or lifted from the baptismal font.

In the resurrection of Jesus Christ,
God has given us a new birth into a living hope.

Rejoice in the good news:
In the name of Jesus Christ, we are forgiven.
Thanks be to God.

PRAYER FOR ILLUMINATION

The prayer for illumination is led from the lectern or pulpit.

> Holy God,
> you are the way, the truth, and the life.
> By the power of your Holy Spirit
> speak your word to us,
> that we might know you more deeply
> and love you more faithfully;
> through Jesus Christ our Savior. **Amen.**

THANKSGIVING FOR BAPTISM

The thanksgiving for baptism is led from the baptismal font.

The introductory dialogue ("The Lord be with you . . .") may be sung or spoken.

> God of the oceans,
> we thank you for the gift of water.
> You wash us clean and renew us;
> you lead us beside still waters and restore our souls.
> You call out for the thirsty to come and drink,
> refreshing us;
> you cause rivers of living water to flow forth from our hearts.
> In the waters of baptism,
> you make us one with Christ
> and join us to each other;
> you pour out your Spirit
> and shower us with gifts.
> Even when we taste the salt of the seas in our own tears,
> you remind us:
> We are baptized. We are not alone. We belong to you.
> All thanks and praise to you,
> fount of every blessing;
> through Jesus Christ our Lord. **Amen.**

GREAT THANKSGIVING

The Great Thanksgiving is led from the Communion table.

The introductory dialogue ("The Lord be with you . . .") may be sung or spoken.

> Holy God, Three-in-One,
> you spoke the world into being
> and breathed your own Spirit into us.
> You have journeyed with us through famines,
> rescued us from oppression,
> and delivered us to freedom.
> Even when we forgot you,
> you did not forget us,
> calling us back through prophets
> and reminding us of your promises.

The Sanctus ("Holy, holy, holy . . .") may be sung or spoken.

> Thank you for your faithfulness
> from generation to generation
> and especially for your Son, Jesus Christ.
> He walks with us along the way
> and makes our hearts burn with his teaching.
> He breaks bread with us
> and opens our eyes to see your grace.
> He anoints us with your healing
> and pours out your love with abandon.

The bread and cup are lifted (but not broken/poured).

> Thank you for this bread of life
> that Jesus blesses and shares,
> his very own body.

> Thank you for this cup of salvation,
> poured out for our forgiveness,
> his very own blood.

A memorial acclamation ("Christ has died . . .") may be sung or spoken.

By the power of your Spirit,
make these gifts a holy meal.
Nourish us, restore us, and equip us
to do your will.
Our hearts and hands are yours, O Lord,
dedicated to your service,
an offering of praise.

Keep us ever faithful until that day
when we will gather at your table in glory,
celebrating with all your children
a feast of endless love.
All honor and praise to you,
holy God, Three-in-One,
now and forever.

A Trinitarian doxology and Great Amen may be sung or spoken.

PRAYER AFTER COMMUNION

The prayer after Communion is led from the Communion table.

Gracious God,
thank you for this feast!
You lay a table for us in the face of all our enemies;
you feed us with the bread of life
and quench our thirst with the wine of gladness.
You nourish us with your presence
and renew our hope in your future.
All thanks and praise to you, O God,
giver of life;
through Jesus Christ our Lord. **Amen.**

PRAYER OF THANKSGIVING

The prayer of thanksgiving may be led from the Communion table.

Creator of all that is,
your earth is full of your gifts.
Your rains water the earth and bring forth food,
and all your creatures praise you.
Your grace flows like the rivers,
and your generosity knows no bounds.
For all that you have given us, thank you.
For all that you have promised us, thank you.
For calling us to share in your goodness
and your work in the world, thank you.
Receive these gifts we bring—
our treasure, our hands, our hearts—
and bless them for the good of your realm;
through Jesus Christ our Lord. **Amen.**

BLESSING

The blessing and charge may be led from the doors of the church.

May God give you the Spirit of wisdom,
confidence in the hope to which you are called,
and the courage to follow Christ wherever he leads. **Alleluia!**

Easter Day/Resurrection of the Lord

Acts 10:34–43 *or*
    Jeremiah 31:1–6
Psalm 118:1–2, 14–24

Colossians 3:1–4 *or* Acts 10:34–43
Matthew 28:1–10 *or* John 20:1–18

OPENING SENTENCES

> Let us take up our tambourines
> and go forth in the dance of the merrymakers!
> **For God's steadfast love endures forever!**
>
> Come, let us go up to Zion, to the Lord our God!
> **Come, let us worship God!**

PRAYER OF THE DAY

> O risen Christ,
> before sending her as the first witness
> to your resurrection glory,
> you revealed to the grieving Mary
> the breadth, the length, the height, and the depth
> of your steadfast love
> with the simple message "Do not be afraid."
> Resurrect in us a bold love
> that overcomes fear
> and sends us to recount what you have done
> through words of comfort,
> catalyzing witness,
> and love of neighbor,
> to the glory of your holy name. **Amen.**

INVITATION TO DISCIPLESHIP

The invitation to discipleship may be led from the baptismal font.

> Beloved children of a loving God,
> in ways big and small,
> we have come to know God's glory.

Will we resist the urge
to hold on tightly to these experiences,
fearing that we might lose them,
as we have lost so much?
Will we witness to God's love with openness,
knowing that the witness of others
may transform us
through God's ongoing revelation?

PRAYERS OF INTERCESSION

The prayers of intercession may be led from the midst of the congregation.

O Christ of great compassion,
in the moments after your resurrection,
you demonstrated your faithful love to Mary,
calling her by name and comforting her fears.
We, too, live in the wake of your risen glory,
still trembling with fear and uncertainty,
even as we trust in your promises.
Hear us now as we call to you;
show us again your steadfast kindness.

O compassionate one,
we pray for those who are surviving the sword,
who face violence of all kinds—
spiritual, emotional, physical, social.
Comfort them,
even as you teach us the ways of wholeness and peace.
Lord, have mercy. **Christ, have mercy.**

O compassionate one,
we pray for those who seek your grace in the wilderness,
who live without a home,
who cry for refuge while in exile,
whose habitats have been destroyed.
Make us into a home for them,
even as you empower us
to address the root causes of rootlessness.
Lord, have mercy. **Christ, have mercy.**

O compassionate one,
we pray for those who long for rest—
rest from grief,
from unjust labor,
from chronic illness,
from anxiety, depression, loneliness, and stress,
from oppression and fear.
Bring them out of the muck and mire
into a broad, still place,
even as you instruct us in the practice of sabbath.
Lord, have mercy. **Christ, have mercy**.

O compassionate one,
we pray for those who only know you from far away,
who have been hurt by the actions
of those who say they love you,
who suffer the kind of doubt that burdens their spirits,
who long to experience your love.
Draw close to them,
even as you shape us into a living embodiment
of your radical welcome.
Lord, have mercy. **Christ, have mercy**.

O Christ of great compassion,
you have loved us with an everlasting love.
Along with all for whom we have already prayed,
we bring before you those prayers left unsaid.
Continue your faithfulness to us,
even as we become more faithful to you;
through the power of your Holy Spirit. **Amen.**

INVITATION TO OFFERING

The invitation to offering may be led from the Communion table.

As those who stand witness
to God's steadfast love,
we are called to follow Christ
in doing good,
healing the oppressed,
and sharing our table.

Let us give of ourselves,
even as God has given to us.

INVITATION TO THE TABLE

The invitation to the table is led from the Communion table.

Peter declared God's impartial invitation,
that "in every nation anyone who fears God
and does what is right is acceptable to God."
Jesus ate and drank with people from all walks of life,
especially those who were considered "sinners" and "outcasts."

This table is open to all
who long for God's wide and grace-filled welcome.
Come, all is prepared.

CHARGE

The blessing and charge may be led from the doors of the church.

God has sent us with a message:
preach peace,
do good,
heal the oppressed,
and testify to forgiveness,
through Jesus' steadfast love.
Amen. *or* **Thanks be to God.**

Easter Evening/ Resurrection of the Lord

Isaiah 25:6–9
Psalm 114

1 Corinthians 5:6b–8
Luke 24:13–49

OPENING SENTENCES

We gather to feast on the joy of new life.
God has swallowed up death forever!

We gather, liberated from the shroud of helplessness.
God has swallowed up death forever!

We gather, a people long expectant,
awaiting restoration no more.
God has swallowed up death forever!

PRAYER OF THE DAY

God of ages long past,
who orders our history and infuses creation with joy,
you have caused mountains to skip like rams,
and hills like lambs.
You have been a sanctuary for your people
and transformed dry places into springs of water.
Gather us now, and in our time together
bind us in the assurance of your history
so that we might be strengthened for your future. **Amen.**

*On this mountain the LORD of hosts will make for all peoples
a feast of rich food, a feast of well-aged wines, of rich food
filled with marrow, of well-aged wines strained clear. And
[God] will destroy on this mountain the shroud that is cast
over all peoples, the sheet that is spread over all nations;
[God] will swallow up death forever.*

Isaiah 25:6–7

INVITATION TO DISCIPLESHIP

The invitation to discipleship may be led from the baptismal font.

As you journey on roads of wonder,
on pathways of disappointment,
on trails of inquiry,
Jesus seeks to walk alongside you.
He calls you to perceive
that which you have been gifted,
the possibilities for which you have been purposed.

You are invited to join with Jesus on the journey,
to see beyond what is seen and to recognize Christ among you,
that you might use your gifts
for the sake of a world
waiting on what you have to offer.

PRAYERS OF INTERCESSION

The prayers of intercession may be led from the midst of the congregation.

Resurrection is here!
Yet we struggle to perceive its presence,
to embrace its significance
for our world and for our lives.
As we join with those saints who came before us
who walked on the road from Jerusalem,
altered by resurrection but wondering what it means,
we offer our prayers and ask God
to help us live in this new reality
that we struggle to fully grasp.

For our world—
transform those governments and corporations that shape it,
that they might be renewed in life-giving purpose
and for the sake of the common good . . .

For our country—
that we might see one another with the renewed insight
of those who have broken bread together
after a long journey on roads of uncertainty . . .

For our church—
that we might find renewal and discover joyful inspiration
through the wondrous inbreaking
of abundant life and life together . . .

For our lives—
that we might lean into the fearful gift of resurrection
with courage and anticipation at what it calls forth from us . . .

God who journeys with us,
continue to open our eyes
so that we may see not only what is possible
but who you call us to be
in the midst of this new possibility.
Strengthen us by our fellowship and communion
with one another and with you,
that we might find sustenance, companionship,
courage, and creativity to walk in your way
as we journey with Jesus. **Amen.**

INVITATION TO OFFERING

The invitation to offering may be led from the Communion table.

Do you not know that a little yeast
leavens the whole batch of dough?
The offerings we give are a symbol of our hope,
a sign of our celebration at what God has done
and what God will do.
Now bring your gifts to lift up this community
and the work of this body.

INVITATION TO THE TABLE

The invitation to the table is led from the Communion table.

As two friends traveled together on the road to Emmaus,
they talked with Jesus.
They wondered aloud at what God was up to,
sharing their hopes and fears,
their dreams and anxieties.
They did not know what was to come,
but they encouraged one another
and found hope in their togetherness.
It was at a table where their eyes were fully opened.

When we gather at this table, you are invited
to come with your own hopes and fears,
your own dreams and anxieties.
Trust and know that Jesus has journeyed with you
on the path that leads here.
Prepare your imaginations now,
that you might encounter what it is
that Jesus is ready to reveal to you
through this meal.

CHARGE

The blessing and charge may be led from the doors of the church.

Go forth from this gathering,
nourished by the fellowship found in broken bread,
strengthened for your journey together,
grounded by Christ's peace, which surpasses understanding,
and inspired to embrace the new reality of resurrection.
Amen. *or* **Thanks be to God.**

Second Sunday of Easter

Acts 2:14a, 22–32   1 Peter 1:3–9
Psalm 16   John 20:19–31

OPENING SENTENCES

The bonds of death could not hold Jesus.
We hid in fear,
but now we are dancing in the streets.

Jesus is not in the tomb.
Jesus is here with us.
We were silent in fear,
but now we are announcing, "Christ is risen!"

PRAYER OF THE DAY

God of life,
from whom all receive their breath,
breathe new life into our tired lungs,
so we may speak words of
faith, hope, and love.
Free us from fear,
that we may follow Christ boldly,
ready to lay down our lives
for your kingdom's cause,
and trusting that you will also
rescue us from the grave
by the power of your Holy Spirit. **Amen.**

---

*Then [Jesus] said to Thomas, "Put your finger here and see my
hands. Reach out your hand and put it in my side. Do not doubt
but believe." Thomas answered him, "My Lord and my God!"*

John 20:27–28

INVITATION TO DISCIPLESHIP

The invitation to discipleship may be led from the baptismal font.

Jesus announces the coming of peace into our lives
and anoints us as peacemakers.
Where there is injustice,
sweat for justice.
Where there is hatred,
embody love.
Where there is brokenness,
see beauty in broken things.

For we have seen and touched
the wounds of Christ:
the nail-pierced hands,
the thorn-pierced head.
We are assured
that our sufferings and services
are not in vain.

PRAYERS OF INTERCESSION

The prayers of intercession may be led from the midst of the congregation.

God, before you
no one is beyond rescue.
In your almighty mercy, **hear our prayer.**

For courage in the church,
that we will be ready to shoulder
any suffering or sacrifice
in order to include more people in your family . . .
In your almighty mercy, **hear our prayer.**

For repentance among the nations,
that they would not be servants of death
but servants of life, seeking peace at any cost . . .
In your almighty mercy, **hear our prayer.**

For unity in our neighborhoods,
that none would be excluded as outsiders
but all might be welcomed as family . . .
In your almighty mercy, **hear our prayer.**

For comfort to those who have lost loved ones . . .
In your almighty mercy, **hear our prayer.**

For justice to those who are trampled on . . .
In your almighty mercy, **hear our prayer.**

For justice to those who trample on the weak . . .
In your almighty mercy, **hear our prayer.**

For courage when we meet our last day . . .
In your almighty mercy, **hear our prayer.**

All this we pray through Jesus Christ,
the conqueror of death. **Amen.**

INVITATION TO OFFERING

The invitation to offering may be led from the Communion table.

Our hearts are glad,
our souls rejoice,
our bodies rest secure—
for God has been exceptionally generous.

So be generous,
and let your gratitude be sincere,
overflowing in gifts for God's work.

INVITATION TO THE TABLE

The invitation to the table is led from the Communion table.

This is the table of the Lord,
where our bodies are nourished
for another day by his sacrifice.

This bread and wine
is life from another
given as life for us—
life from Christ,
so we can live for Christ.
Here we eat and drink,
keenly aware that our life
is never our own.

CHARGE

The blessing and charge may be led from the doors of the church.

Death's sting has been removed.
Jesus has shattered the grave;
now there is a whole new world.
Go and broadcast this good news:
the days of death and death's minions—
fear, injustice, and hoarding—
are done forever.
Amen. *or* **Thanks be to God.**

Third Sunday of Easter

Acts 2:14a, 36–41
Psalm 116:1–4, 12–19

1 Peter 1:17–23
Luke 24:13–35

OPENING SENTENCES

I love the Lord!
**Because God has heard me
and not ignored my cry.**

God has saved my life repeatedly!
**So my life belongs to God.
I am God's child,
happy to sing of God's work in me.**

PRAYER OF THE DAY

Loving God,
you ransomed us from futility
with the precious blood of Christ.
We can hardly believe
how precious we are to you!
Holy Spirit, help us to believe this truth
fully with our whole life:
flesh, bone, and spirit. **Amen.**

---

*Peter said to them, "Repent, and be baptized every one of you
in the name of Jesus Christ so that your sins may be forgiven;
and you will receive the gift of the Holy Spirit. For the
promise is for you, for your children, and for all who are far
away, everyone whom the Lord our God calls to him."*

Acts 2:38–39

INVITATION TO DISCIPLESHIP

The invitation to discipleship may be led from the baptismal font.

God bought us at the priceless cost of Christ's blood.
We belong to God.
All of our lives: past, present, and future.

So let us offer up our lives
completely and without conditions.
God's truth is our North Star,
God's love shapes our actions,
God's faith dismisses cynicism.
Christ's resurrection is our reality.

PRAYERS OF INTERCESSION

The prayers of intercession may be led from the midst of the congregation.

If God did not spare Jesus for our lives,
then God will not dismiss our prayers.
Therefore, with confidence we pray.
We pray for the church . . .
that we would remember our commissioning:
how you breathed your Holy Spirit into us
and empowered us for the work of reconciliation.

We pray for our world . . .
that we would seek life over death,
repentance over self-righteousness,
forgiveness over vengeance,
justice over racism.

We pray for our community . . .
that we would seek truth over myths,
vulnerability over security,
peace over passivity.

We pray for our loved ones . . .
that we would seek trust over cynicism,
love over pity,
intimacy over isolation,
hope over despair.

Meet us today, resurrected Lord.
Lead us to live in a world
where you have defeated death
and defeatism. **Amen.**

INVITATION TO OFFERING

The invitation to offering may be led from the Communion table.

God gave us Christ.
Should we hold back anything from God?
Christ gave us the Holy Spirit.
Should we hold back anything from God?

Let us give generously,
even giving our own lives,
as God has given us everything already.

INVITATION TO THE TABLE

The invitation to the table is led from the Communion table.

When the disciples broke bread,
their eyes were opened to see
that the stranger they had invited for dinner
was none other than their friend Jesus.

Today as we break bread,
open your eyes.
The person next to you
is none other than our friend Jesus.
**Jesus, we thank you
for inviting us to meet you
at this table.**

CHARGE

The blessing and charge may be led from the doors of the church.

Is there any more important news
than the fact that Jesus is alive
and you have met the Lord?
Go and tell everyone.
Tell it with your lips and with your life.
Love, forgive, and share
as one who is no longer afraid of death.
Amen. *or* **Thanks be to God.**

Fourth Sunday of Easter

Acts 2:42–47   1 Peter 2:19–25
Psalm 23   John 10:1–10

OPENING SENTENCES

> Praise God, the Good Shepherd.
> **In the valley's deep shadows,**
> **God's voice guides us.**
>
> We are God's sheep,
> **and God never abandons God's own sheep.**

PRAYER OF THE DAY

> God, your loving voice calls us.
> With our names spoken so tenderly,
> we follow joyfully.
> Jesus, when we lose our way,
> you don't give up until
> you have us securely in your arms.
> Holy Spirit, help us express
> our soul's deep desire
> to meet you in worship today. **Amen.**

INVITATION TO DISCIPLESHIP

The invitation to discipleship may be led from the baptismal font.

> Jesus' resurrection is an act of new creation.
> The church is Jesus' first vision of new creation.
>
> So invite people into your homes,
> those cast aside by the world.
> Open your hands;
> do not let your possessions possess you,
> but share them with those who really need them.
> Live freely
> in this new world of God's love.

PRAYERS OF INTERCESSION

The prayers of intercession may be led from the midst of the congregation.

Jesus, the Good Shepherd, came to give us life—
and not just any life, but abundant life.
So let us never hesitate to ask from Jesus
good things for all people.
Good Shepherd,
in your great love for us, **hear our prayer.**

For your church in all the world . . .
that we would be a community with open doors,
not reflecting divisions in our community
but shattering them with open tables.
In your great love for us, **hear our prayer.**

For the leaders of nations . . .
that they would fear your judgment,
knowing that the people under their watch
first belong to you,
the Great Shepherd of all people.
In your great love for us, **hear our prayer.**

For the earth you have made—
the prairies, the valleys,
the mountains, the oceans . . .
that we might be good stewards of them,
tending to them as you tend to us so tenderly.
In your great love for us, **hear our prayer.**

For the poor who are ignored . . .
that they may know they are God's image bearers
and that we may know they are God's image bearers.
In your great love for us, **hear our prayer.**

For migrants and refugees . . .
that, though they might be without a nation,
they may know they are not without a God
and an advocate.
In your great love for us, **hear our prayer.**

Good Shepherd,
in your great love for us, **hear our prayer. Amen.**

INVITATION TO OFFERING

The invitation to offering may be led from the Communion table.

We give because we are abundantly blessed.
We are given more than we need,
so we can give to those in need.

We give joyfully and humbly,
knowing we are simply following
the way Jesus gave himself to us.

INVITATION TO THE TABLE

The invitation to the table is led from the Communion table.

This is the table of the Lord.
Enemies are reconciled and made family.
Strangers grow to be friends.
And humans come to call themselves
friends of God.

This the table of the Lord.
We do not choose who gets to come,
because we are all guests,
fortunate to be invited.
The Lord is the host.
We are happy to be with everyone at the table.

Come and enjoy this great feast
hosted by the great God.

CHARGE

The blessing and charge may be led from the doors of the church.

You have never been alone.
Now go, whether before you
is a prairie or a valley.
You don't go alone.
The Good Shepherd
is with you, guiding you,
feeding you,
even carrying you
on strong shoulders.
Go in peace.
Amen. *or* **Thanks be to God.**

Fifth Sunday of Easter

Acts 7:55–60   1 Peter 2:2–10
Psalm 31:1–5, 15–16   John 14:1–14

OPENING SENTENCES

God is our rock and refuge!
**Nothing can shake me
from God's steadfast love.**

Our God is a fortress of justice!
**No weapons of oppression
can loosen a single brick!**

PRAYER OF THE DAY

God, the great architect,
designing a world where no one is left out:
You established Jesus as the cornerstone
for a temple where the Holy Spirit roams freely,
going forth to all people.
Redesign our churches and nations
to imitate your heavenly temple,
where there is no center and no margin.
Begin by redesigning our hearts
as we worship you this day. **Amen.**

---

*Come to [the Lord], a living stone, though rejected by mortals
yet chosen and precious in God's sight, and like living stones,
let yourselves be built into a spiritual house, to be a holy
priesthood, to offer spiritual sacrifices acceptable to God
through Jesus Christ.*

1 Peter 2:4–5

INVITATION TO DISCIPLESHIP

The invitation to discipleship may be led from the baptismal font.

You are a chosen people,
a royal priesthood,
a holy nation,
selected by God from the start!

Pray for the world,
stand in the gap.
From the weak, learn strength.
From the poor, learn abundance.
From the meek, learn obedience.
From the rejected, learn God's acceptance.

PRAYERS OF INTERCESSION

The prayers of intercession may be led from the midst of the congregation.

We are holy priests.
As Jesus intercedes for us,
we intercede for the world.
In your mercy, **hear our prayer.**

We stand with the church . . .
When we forget that we are your holy people—
that our obedience is to you and not the nations—
help us to remember our loyalty.
In your mercy, **hear our prayer.**

We stand with all the families of the earth . . .
For those who are suffering,
help us to lend our shoulders.
For those who cause suffering,
help them to see that our lives are interwoven.
For all of us who suffer and cause suffering,
grant us comfort and conviction.
In your mercy, **hear our prayer.**

We stand with all creatures of the earth,
plants and animals, amoebas, and whales,
remembering all creation . . .
As those called to be stewards of creation,
we repent of our negligence
and the ways in which we misappropriate creation
for our benefit alone.
Help us to practice compassionate responsibility,
knowing that our care for the earth
is a form of obedience to our calling
as your holy people.
In your mercy, **hear our prayer.**

O God, let our prayers
give voice to your desire for all creatures.
As your royal priesthood,
help us express more fully and faithfully
your holy will. **Amen.**

INVITATION TO OFFERING

The invitation to offering may be led from the Communion table.

God desires our offerings—
not because God is in need,
but so we can experience
the joy of God's pleasure.
**We bring our gifts
as people who are madly in love
with the God whose love is beyond speech.**

INVITATION TO THE TABLE

The invitation to the table is led from the Communion table.

Jesus invites us to the table as siblings,
though we were once traitors.
We are welcomed as God's priests,
though once we were without mercy and merciless.

Once we were not God's people;
now we are God's treasure.
Once we were sinners;
now we are called saints.
We are still faithless,
but God remains faithful.
We are speechless before God's love
so visible around this table.

CHARGE

The blessing and charge may be led from the doors of the church.

As God's people,
you are God's message of love to the lonely.
You are Christ's zeal for justice to the oppressed.
You are the nail-scarred hands of Christ to the doubters.
Don't shirk away from your great commission.
Live up to your identity.
God is always with you.
Amen. *or* **Thanks be to God.**

Sixth Sunday of Easter

Acts 17:22–31   1 Peter 3:13–22
Psalm 66:8–20   John 14:15–21

OPENING SENTENCES

Jesus said, "If you love me,
you will keep my commandments."
Risen Lord,
give us your Advocate,
the Spirit of truth,
to abide in us as we abide in you.

Jesus said, "I will not leave you orphaned;
I am coming to you."
Risen Lord,
we will watch for your coming.
Because you live,
we will live in you.

PRAYER OF THE DAY

You alone, O Lord,
are the Maker of heaven and earth.
In you we live and move and have our being.
We are your children,
and you are our God.
Teach us to turn away from false idols
and to turn to you in faith;
through Jesus Christ our Savior,
who is risen from the dead. **Amen.**

INVITATION TO DISCIPLESHIP

The invitation to discipleship may be led from the baptismal font.

In the days of Noah,
the time of the great flood,
God saved eight persons through the ark.

Now salvation is offered to all
through the water of baptism
and the gift of the church—
a ship of faith on stormy seas.

Come and share this journey with us.
Come and find refuge from the flood
in the grace of Jesus Christ our Savior.

PRAYERS OF INTERCESSION

The prayers of intercession may be led from the midst of the congregation.

Blessed are you, O God,
for you have kept us among the living;
you did not let our feet slip.

We pray for those we love . . .
Help those who are suffering,
and deliver those who are in trouble
to find new life and hope in you.

We pray for our community . . .
Be with our neighbors
who are passing through fire and flood,
and bring them out into a place of peace.

We pray for nations and leaders . . .
Teach them to do what is right,
without fear or intimidation,
and to seek the welfare of all people.

We pray for the church . . .
Let your Holy Spirit abide in us
and lead us in keeping the commandments
of Jesus Christ our Savior.

We pray for creation . . .
Give life and breath and wholeness
to all the creatures of the world,
for you are the Lord of heaven and earth.

Blessed are you, O God,
for you receive our prayers
and keep us in your steadfast love;
through Jesus Christ our Lord. **Amen.**

INVITATION TO OFFERING

The invitation to offering may be led from the Communion table.

Here, in the house of the Lord,
we present our offerings
to the one who has delivered us from death
and welcomed us into eternal life.

Let us bring before the Holy One
our offerings of thanks and praise.

INVITATION TO THE TABLE

The invitation to the table is led from the Communion table.

This table is not an altar
"to an unknown god."
This is the table of the one true God,
who made the heavens and earth.
This is the table of Jesus Christ,
whom we know as Savior and Lord.
This is the table of the Holy Spirit,
who knows us through and through.

Come to this table,
where you are known
as God's beloved child.

CHARGE

The blessing and charge may be led from the doors of the church.

Let us be eager to do good
and always ready to share
the hope that is within us.
Amen. *or* **Thanks be to God.**

Ascension of the Lord

Acts 1:1–11
Psalm 47 *or* Psalm 93

Ephesians 1:15–23
Luke 24:44–53

OPENING SENTENCES

Clap your hands, all you peoples.
Jesus is risen from the dead!

Shout to God with songs of joy.
Jesus has ascended into heaven!

Sing praises to God, all the earth.
Jesus will come again to reign!

PRAYER OF THE DAY

O Lord our God,
you have called us to bear witness
to your saving work in the world
through the dying and rising
of Jesus Christ our Savior.
Now make us ready to receive
the gift of your Holy Spirit
so that all may know and trust
the promise of your holy word.
In Jesus' name we pray. **Amen.**

INVITATION TO DISCIPLESHIP

The invitation to discipleship may be led from the baptismal font.

The power of God is at work in you—
opening the eyes of your heart,
calling you to live in hope,
claiming you as God's beloved.

How great is the power of God
for those who come to believe.

PRAYERS OF INTERCESSION

The prayers of intercession may be led from the midst of the congregation.

With faith in the Lord Jesus Christ
and love for the people of God,
we remember all these things in prayer:

We pray for the world . . .
Restore the majesty and beauty of the earth
so that all creation reveals your glory;
through Jesus Christ our Lord. **Amen.**

We pray for the church . . .
Open our minds to understand your word,
and open our hearts to love and serve you;
through Jesus Christ our Lord. **Amen.**

We pray for our neighbors . . .
Help us to live in peace with one another
and to show compassion to those in need;
through Jesus Christ our Lord. **Amen.**

We pray for our loved ones . . .
Heal the sick, comfort those who suffer,
and give life to all who call on you;
through Jesus Christ our Lord. **Amen.**

As you have put your power to work in Christ,
O God, work out your purpose in us,
proclaiming the gospel to all
and raising the dead to life.
All this we pray in the name of Jesus—
the name above every name,
the ruler of creation,
and the head of the church,
now and always. **Amen.**

INVITATION TO OFFERING

The invitation to offering may be led from the Communion table.

We have a glorious inheritance in Jesus Christ—
the immeasurable gift of God's grace.

With great thanksgiving
let us offer our lives to the Lord.

INVITATION TO THE TABLE

The invitation to the table is led from the Communion table.

The Lord be with you. **And also with you.**

At this heavenly banquet,
by the power of the Holy Spirit
we are lifted into the presence
of the Lord Jesus Christ,
who is seated at the right hand of God.

Therefore we gather at this table, saying:
Lift up your hearts. **We lift them to the Lord.**

Let us give thanks to the Lord our God.
It is right to give our thanks and praise.

The Great Thanksgiving continues . . .

CHARGE

The blessing and charge may be led from the doors of the church.

We are witnesses to these things:
Jesus is risen from the dead!
Jesus has ascended into heaven!
Jesus will come again to reign!
Amen. *or* **Thanks be to God.**

Seventh Sunday of Easter

Acts 1:6–14
Psalm 68:1–10, 32–35

1 Peter 4:12–14; 5:6–11
John 17:1–11

OPENING SENTENCES

Let the righteous be joyful;
let them be jubilant before God.
**Sing to God, sing praises
to the name of the Lord.**

Lift up a song to the Lord,
who rides upon the clouds.
**God is the parent of orphans
and the protector of those who mourn.**

Awesome is God in the sanctuary;
the Lord gives power and strength to the people.
Blessed be the Lord!

PRAYER OF THE DAY

Make us one, O God, as you are one.
Show us the gift of eternal life:
to know you as you know us.
Help us to finish the work
that you have called us to do,
that we may glorify you always;
through Jesus Christ our Lord. **Amen.**

[Jesus] looked up to heaven and said, "Father, the hour has come; glorify your Son so that the Son may glorify you, since you have given him authority over all people, to give eternal life to all whom you have given him. And this is eternal life, that they may know you, the only true God, and Jesus Christ whom you have sent."

John 17:1b–3

INVITATION TO DISCIPLESHIP

The invitation to discipleship may be led from the baptismal font.

Beloved ones, do not be surprised
at the fiery ordeal taking place.
Rejoice in the sufferings of Christ,
that you may shout for joy
when the glory of God is revealed.
The Spirit of God, the Spirit of glory,
is resting on you.

God is calling you
to be a disciple of Jesus Christ.
How will you respond?

PRAYERS OF INTERCESSION

The prayers of intercession may be led from the midst of the congregation.

Rise up, O God,
and scatter the enemies of sin and death.
Hear our prayer.

We pray for those we love . . .
Restore them to health and peace,
that they may know fullness of life
in your abundant mercy.

We pray for our community . . .
Support those who are struggling
for fair wages, housing, and health care,
that they may have all they need.

We pray for nations and leaders . . .
Strengthen their resolve
to pursue peace instead of war,
that all may live in safety.

We pray for the church . . .
Establish your holy people
as a sign of what you intend
for all the world.

We pray for creation . . .
Discipline us to be good stewards
of the resources of the earth,
that future generations may know your glory.

Pour out your mercy, O God,
to provide for those in need.
Send out your mighty voice
to establish justice in the earth.
Give power to your people,
that we may bless your holy name. **Amen.**

INVITATION TO OFFERING

The invitation to offering may be led from the Communion table.

Through faith in Christ Jesus
we have come to share
in the life and love of the eternal God.

Let us glorify the Lord
with the offering of our lives.

INVITATION TO THE TABLE

The invitation to the table is led from the Communion table.

The disciples asked Jesus,
"Lord, is this the time
when you will restore the kingdom?"
Jesus replied, "You will receive power
when the Holy Spirit has come upon you;
and you will be my witnesses . . .
to the ends of the earth."

Now is the time
for the feast of the kingdom.
The Holy Spirit is coming.
Let us gather at the table of the Lord.

CHARGE

The blessing and charge may be led from the doors of the church.

Rejoice when you share in Christ's suffering.
Humble yourself under God's mighty hand.
Cast your anxiety on God, who cares for you.
Resist the evil one, and be steadfast in your faith.
The God of all grace, who has called you to glory,
will restore, support, strengthen, and establish you.
Amen. *or* **Thanks be to God.**

Day of Pentecost

Acts 2:1–21 *or*
    Numbers 11:24–30
Psalm 104:24–34, 35b

1 Corinthians 12:3b–13 *or* Acts 2:1–21
John 20:19–23 *or* John 7:37–39

OPENING SENTENCES

Come, Holy Spirit!
Grant us your peace.

Come, Holy Spirit!
Give us your power.

Come, Holy Spirit!
Grace us with your presence.

Let us worship God.

PRAYER OF THE DAY

Holy One, you sent your Spirit
to lead us in the paths of peace.
Breathe into us
the voice of prophecy.
Breathe into us
the power of forgiveness.
Breathe into us
the gifts of ministry,
that we may serve your people;
through Jesus Christ our Lord. **Amen.**

INVITATION TO DISCIPLESHIP

The invitation to discipleship may be led from the baptismal font.

There are varieties of gifts,
but the same Spirit.
There are varieties of services,
but the same Lord.

There are varieties of activities,
but it is the same God
who activates them in everyone.

How will you use your gifts
in the service of God?

PRAYERS OF INTERCESSION

The prayers of intercession may be led from the midst of the congregation.

O Lord, send forth your Spirit
to renew the face of the earth.
Hear our prayers.

We pray for those we love . . .
Pour out your Holy Spirit
on those who are suffering,
that they may know healing and mercy.

We pray for our community . . .
Fill us with dreams and visions
of the world as you desire,
that all may have enough.

We pray for nations and leaders . . .
Reveal to them your wisdom,
and guide them in your ways,
that they may seek justice and peace.

We pray for the church . . .
Inspire us by your word,
and activate us in your service,
that we may use our gifts for good.

We pray for creation . . .
Give to all creatures
their food in due season,
that they may look to you and live.

O Lord, may your glory endure forever.
Teach us to seek your will
and sing your praise
as long as we live;
through Christ our Lord. **Amen.**

INVITATION TO OFFERING

The invitation to offering may be led from the Communion table.

The Spirit of God is given to each one of us—
with wisdom, knowledge, and faith;
through healing, miracles, and prophecy;
in discernment, speaking, and interpretation.

With gratitude for the gifts of the Spirit,
let us offer our lives to the Lord.

INVITATION TO THE TABLE

The invitation to the table is led from the Communion table.

Jesus says,
"Let anyone who is thirsty come to me,
and let the one who believes in me drink.
Out of the believer's heart
shall flow rivers of living water."

If you are thirsty for the grace of God,
come to the table.
Trust in the one who gives us
the bread of life and living water,
that we may never hunger and thirst again.

CHARGE

The blessing and charge may be led from the doors of the church.

Receive the Holy Spirit.
Go forth in peace,
and share the peace of Christ with all.
Amen. *or* **Thanks be to God.**

Supplements for the
Narrative Lectionary

Matthew 1:1–17

Narrative Lectionary Year 1, 19 (Christmas 1)
(with Psalm 132:11–12)

See also the resources for the First Sunday after Christmas Day.

OPENING SENTENCES

> From Abraham to David,
> from Josiah to Joseph,
> **the word of God endures forever.**
>
> Through Tamar and Rahab,
> through Ruth and Bathsheba,
> **the word of God endures forever.**
>
> From covenant to kingdom,
> through exile and expectation,
> **the word of God endures forever.**
>
> Let us worship God.

PRAYER OF THE DAY

> God of our ancestors,
> from generation to generation
> you have showed your saving love
> and holy purpose for your people.
> Gather us together and keep us
> in that great cloud of witnesses,
> that we may proclaim the good news
> of Jesus the Messiah. **Amen.**

INVITATION TO DISCIPLESHIP

The invitation to discipleship may be led from the baptismal font.

In every age, God calls us
to step forth in faith,
to offer our worship and service,
and to live by the Word.

How will you be a part
of the great story of salvation?
How will you proclaim
the past promises of God
to present and future generations?
Join us in this journey of discipleship.

PRAYERS OF INTERCESSION

The prayers of intercession may be led from the midst of the congregation.

O Lord our God,
through long generations
you have redeemed your people
in their times of distress.
Hear our prayers for the world.
Lord, in your mercy, **hear our prayer.**

Deliver those who are in trouble . . .
Lord, in your mercy, **hear our prayer.**

Give rest to those who are weary . . .
Lord, in your mercy, **hear our prayer.**

Give shelter to those without homes . . .
Lord, in your mercy, **hear our prayer.**

Bless the poor with abundance . . .
Lord, in your mercy, **hear our prayer.**

Satisfy the hungry with bread . . .
Lord, in your mercy, **hear our prayer.**

Keep us faithful as your people . . .
Lord, in your mercy, **hear our prayer.**

Rise up, O Lord,
and show us your glory,
your righteousness, justice, and peace.
Then we will shout for joy
in the company of the faithful.
Then we will sing with gladness
the good news of salvation;
through Jesus the Messiah. **Amen.**

INVITATION TO OFFERING

The invitation to offering may be led from the Communion table.

Give thanks to God, who has enabled us
to share in the inheritance of all the saints
through the grace of the Lord Jesus Christ.

With gratitude for God's grace,
let us offer our lives and gifts to the Lord.

INVITATION TO THE TABLE

The invitation to the table is led from the Communion table.

As the Lord God came to Abraham and Sarah,
sharing a meal with them under the oak trees,
God is here with us.

As the Lord God came to David, the shepherd king,
spreading a table in the wilderness,
God is here with us.

As the Lord Jesus Christ was born in Bethlehem,
making his bed in a feeding trough,
God is here with us.

Come to the table of the Lord.

CHARGE

The blessing and charge may be led from the doors of the church.

Our ancestors waited for this day.
Tell the good news to all:
Jesus the Messiah is with us.
Amen. *or* **Thanks be to God.**

Matthew 18:1–9

Narrative Lectionary Year 1, 30 (Ash Wednesday)
(with Psalm 146:7c–10 or Psalm 51:1–3)

See also the resources for Ash Wednesday.

OPENING SENTENCES

> The Lord sets prisoners free
> and opens the eyes of the blind.
> **The Lord lifts up the oppressed**
> **and loves the righteous.**
>
> The Lord watches over strangers
> and upholds orphans and widows,
> **but God brings to ruin**
> **the way of the wicked.**
>
> The Lord will reign forever.
> **Praise the Lord!**

PRAYER OF THE DAY

> Holy God, in Christ you set before us
> your way of truth and life.
> As we begin our Lenten journey,
> remove the stumbling blocks before us,
> so that we may follow you faithfully
> all the way to the cross;
> through Jesus Christ our Lord. **Amen.**

INVITATION TO DISCIPLESHIP

The invitation to discipleship may be led from the baptismal font.

Who is the greatest in the kingdom of God?
Jesus says it is the one who comes as a child.
Unless we become like children
we will never enter the kingdom of God.

Come to God, then, as beloved children.
Jesus welcomes your questions
and delights in your first steps of faith.
Jesus welcomes you.

PRAYERS OF INTERCESSION

The prayers of intercession may be led from the midst of the congregation.

O Lord our God, show us your will,
and help us to seek your way.

When leaders and people are divided,
teach us to seek the common good.

When loved ones are separated or isolated,
hold us together in your embrace.

When neighbors are struggling to survive,
show us how to provide for all in need.

When hatred and fear lead to violence,
bring justice and reconciliation to our land.

When the church is slow to speak and act,
help us to welcome your prophetic word.

Fulfill our prayers, O Lord our God,
and guide us to fulfill your purpose;
in the name of Christ our Savior. **Amen.**

INVITATION TO OFFERING

The invitation to offering may be led from the Communion table.

The sacrifice acceptable to God is a broken spirit;
a broken and contrite heart God will not despise.

Let us offer our lives to the God of grace.

INVITATION TO THE TABLE

The invitation to the table is led from the Communion table.

This is the table of abundant mercy.
This is the table of steadfast love.
The hungry and thirsty are welcome here.
Orphans and widows are welcome here.
Sinners and strangers are welcome here.

God welcomes you,
God washes you clean,
God prepares a place of honor for you
at this table of grace.

CHARGE

The blessing and charge may be led from the doors of the church.

Come to Christ as a child,
and you will enter the kingdom of heaven.
Welcome others in Christ's name,
and you will welcome the Lord.
Amen. *or* **Thanks be to God.**

Scripture Index

This is an index to the lectionary readings supported in this volume. Revised Common Lectionary readings are listed in regular type; supplemental readings for the Narrative Lectionary are listed in italics.

Contributors

CLAUDIA L. AGUILAR RUBALCAVA, Pastor, First Mennonite Church, Denver

MAMIE BROADHURST, Co-Pastor, University Presbyterian Church, Baton Rouge, Louisiana

DAVID GAMBRELL, Associate for Worship, Office of Theology and Worship, Presbyterian Mission Agency, Presbyterian Church (U.S.A.), Louisville, Kentucky

MARCI AULD GLASS, Pastor and Head of Staff, Calvary Presbyterian Church, San Francisco

MARCUS A. HONG, Director of Field Education and Assistant Professor of Practical Theology, Louisville Presbyterian Theological Seminary, Louisville, Kentucky

KIMBERLY BRACKEN LONG, Liturgical Scholar, Cambridge, Maryland

EMILY McGINLEY, Senior Pastor, City Church, San Francisco

SAMUEL SON, Manager of Diversity and Reconciliation, Executive Director's Office, Presbyterian Mission Agency, Presbyterian Church (U.S.A.), Louisville, Kentucky

SLATS TOOLE, Freelance Writer, Minneapolis

BYRON A. WADE, General Presbyter, Presbytery of Western North Carolina, Morganton, North Carolina